Rough and Tumble

Rough and Tumble

By

Bob Roberts

Illustrated

Seafarer Books

2003

© Sheila Roberts 2003

First published in the UK by:-
Sampson Low and Marston 1935
2nd Edition Mallard Reprints, Lavenham Press 1983

This edition:-
Seafarer Books
102 Redwald Road
Rendlesham
Woodbridge
Suffolk IP12 2TE

UK ISBN 0 9538180 9 8

Typesetting and design by Julie Beadle
Cover design by Louis Mackay
Drawings by Louis Roskell
Photographs by Bob Roberts arranged by Louis Mackay

British Library Cataloguing in Publication Data

Roberts, Bob, 1907-1982
    Rough and tumble. – 3rd ed.
    1. Roberts, Bob, 1907-1982 – Journeys – Costa Rica – Cocos
    Island 2. Cocos Island (Costa Rica) – Description and travel
    I. Title
    910. 4'5'092

ISBN 0953818098

Printed in Finland by W. S. Bookwell OY

To Jack
Brigadier (Retired) J. C. Govier, C.B.E.,
A lifelong friend of the author

Illustrations

And thus the great adventure was decided upon.
(Inset: Bob and Bully in even younger days.)

Thelma on the Thames off Erith

We found that by eating less we did not feel so much the craving for water. Picture taken with an elastic band.
We crossed over to Algeciras to see the famous bullfighters at Seville

Jimmy Riddle, third member of the ship's company after Port of Spain

Shark – food to augment our stores

At Balboa. We took care to put a band of copper paint above the Muntz metal sheathing
Thelma coming through the Panama Canal alongside *Avance*
The last of *Thelma*, with her starboard side ripped out on the rocks of Cocos island

Cooknell's shelter on Cocos island, made from an old sail
Exploring ashore
Sam, in happier mood
The bluenose schooner, Franklin Barnett

Contents

Introduction

In 1923, as a 15 year old schoolboy, Bob Roberts shipped out in the barquentine *Waterwitch* from Poole in Dorset. Fifty-five years later, in 1978, he stepped ashore for the last time from the motor coaster *Vectis Isle* at Newport on the Isle of Wight. During these years of seafaring, many other interests held his attention. At various times he was a journalist, author, broadcaster, singer of sea songs, athlete and cricketer. Also a boxer, following one fight when the punters were throwing their coins into the ring, his mentor, Gypsy Daniels, offered some sound advice, 'don't look so pleased when you win lad, just pick up the money.'

An adventurer, as this story recalls, Bob always appeared to stand four-square, with strong shoulders and large hands. Both afloat and ashore he took his time to weigh up people he met, until a trust developed for those he came to respect, which very often lasted a lifetime. Perhaps not so well known was the gift that he possessed for dealing with delinquents who came his way and who were living on the edge. By gentle example and encouragement he was able to bring them back into line.

Experience of life, gained after years at sea, was his in large measure. With the barge *Cambria*, Bob was the last to trade and carry cargo in European waters in a vessel under sail only. Now just a footnote to our maritime history. Scribbled in the back of an old almanac, in Bob's hand, was written:

'Gone now all those beautiful vessels and very many of their masters and crews and the world is the worse of it.'

As a generous friend and as a fellow seafarer, it has been my privilege to have enjoyed the company of Bob Roberts.

Richard May. (Master Mariner)

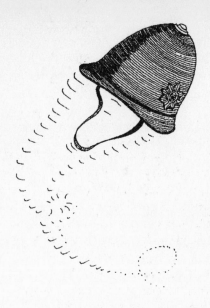

North Sea Shake-down

"Watch-o."

The never-welcome call brought me from my bunk as the first grey streaks of dawn broke over the North Sea. I pulled on my seaboots in the befuddled state of a man who has long been trying, unsuccessfully, to make up his hours of sleep to the customary requirements of nature.

It was a wild morning and I knew by the violent, labouring motion of our little vessel that she was not taking things too well. I could hear the noise of the spray as it splashed on the deck above and had to hang on grimly as I lurched towards the cabin door.

"How's the weather?" I called to the helmsman as I struggled into my oilskins and sou'wester.

"Bloody awful."

And with this enlightening remark Arthur Frank Bull left me in charge of the tiller and rolled up in the warm blankets I had so reluctantly vacated.

The cutter *Thelma* was only 26 feet 10 inches in length, with 8 feet 3 inches of beam and 5 feet draught; yet, sturdy West Country smack though she was, the weather was already too bad to hope that she would get into the port of Den Helder to shelter and safety before the gale reached its height. The seas were so steep that one experienced a giddy sensation when sliding down into the troughs and an anxious feeling when she bravely climbed the next wave.

We were homeward bound to London River from Emden in Germany. Somewhere to seaward was the Terschelling lightship. To the south-east were the low-lying Frisian Islands, with dangerous shoals extending several miles offshore. We could not see, either; and little wonder, for a cloud of spray blew from one wave top to another and limited our range of vision to two or three hundred yards, even when we were poised on a crest.

I had been at the tiller but half an hour when I determined that the time had come to heave-to. Even had it been possible to get the vessel before the wind I had no charts of the narrow channels between the islands which might have led us to calmer water.

She was already under close-reefed canvas, and I pulled the jib sheet a'weather and let her lie-to. I could then crouch under the lee of the cabin bulkhead, smoke my pipe and reflect on what a fool I was to be caught in a gale in such a notoriously bad spot as this. A fool to be at sea at all, perhaps, but that at least is open to argument.

One of the crew (there were three of us) thought it foolish and said so. He was a cockney named Begbie, and I think his opinion was influenced by the fact that as he emerged from the cabin to come on watch at eight o'clock he was just in time to catch a large amount of North Sea in the back of the neck. No sooner had Begbie taken over the watch than there was a loud crack forward, followed by a ripping and tearing of canvas. The jib had blown to pieces.

I crawled forward along the weather side. It was impossible to stand up like a human being, and I felt much more like a baboon as I hung on to the mast and bitts to get the remnants inboard. They would have flogged the masthead off had we left them there, and so I managed to get a reefed foresail set before further damage was done.

For eight hours *Thelma* rode the storm without giving us cause for anxiety and my confidence in her increased rapidly. I began to feel proud of her, for I had bought her only a few months before. This was a trial trip, the first development of two years' planning. What the trial was for the other two did not know. For them it was nothing more than a sailing trip up the Dutch coast as far as the River Ems. But for me it was different. It was the beginning of the "great adventure".

However carefully one chooses a small vessel to go to sea in, it is never quite certain what she will do until she meets with the worst of conditions. For this reason I felt almost pleased that this foul weather had swooped down on us and given *Thelma* a chance to show me her qualities.

Just as I was beginning to revel in the battle an ominous slit appeared in the leech of the mainsail. Had it extended across the sail it would have spelt the doom of both *Thelma* and her crew, for without some canvas abaft the mast she could not hope to ride such a wicked sea.

Begbie was quick to see the danger. He sprang to the bulwarks and hauled down the leech line to close the gap while Bully and I grabbed his legs and held him from being pitched overboard.

After eight hours it seemed that the gale might blow out before the day was done. We prayed that it might, as we were tired, drenched and very hungry. It was impossible to cook and all we could do was nibble cheese and drink water. We took turns to stretch out on the cabin floor, wedged in by a sack of potatoes, for it was no longer possible to keep within the narrow limits of a bunk. Bully was crudely awakened during his spell below by the clock flying from its proper resting place and opening a gash in his head. All three of us were repeatedly thrown down and bruised.

Once a great Dutch schooner loomed up on our weather bow, scudding before the wind like a wild thing heading straight for us. I saw two figures struggling at her wheel. We could do nothing to get out of her way. All we could do was hang on to the cockpit coaming and watch. I think we were all privately contemplating what we should do if the schooner his us when a third figure ran to the wheel and the vessel answered. She tore past our stern and rounded up into the wind a mile to leeward of us, backing her headsails and lying-to the same as we were. Even then she drove to leeward so rapidly that within an hour we lost sight of her. Unless she got through one of the inter-island channels she must have struck the shoals of Vlieland and gone to her doom.

Late in the afternoon we saw land ourselves. It was a low dark streak to the southward, little more than a mud bank and perhaps only a couple of miles away. With such bad visibility it was impossible to tell how near we were or how fast the *Thelma* was being blown towards it. To my great relief the weather had begun to show signs of moderating and we let draw and got the vessel on the other tack.

We did our best to sail away from the land, but it was two hours before we could be certain that we were even holding our own. *Thelma* reared and bucked, buried her rail and looked like being hove down flat in the squalls. But she held on, and gradually that grim streak to leeward was lost to view.

The danger was over. That night the wind eased to a pleasant breeze and two days later we were snugly berthed at Helder with the beautiful old fishing boats of the Zuider Zee.

By way of a breather we made a leisurely journey to Amsterdam by canal, and on to Ymuiden, there to pick up a spanking north-easterly breeze to carry us back to England.

Our first cruise in the *Thelma* over, we returned to our respective jobs: I to a stuffy haunt in Fleet Street and Bully to the duties of a policeman in the wilds of North London. Begbie left us to join another vessel on the south coast.

One night, an evil, foggy night when the streets of London look at their very worst, Bully and I held counsel over a pint of foaming ale in a riverside tavern.

"Bully," I said, "how would you like to chuck up the police and go on a long cruise in the *Thelma*?"

Bully (I find it difficult to write of him by any other name) sighed and shrugged his massive shoulders.

"Wish I could."

I then unfolded to him the cruise I had been dreaming of for the past two years, during which I had been penned up by common necessity in the morbid shadows of Fleet Street. I had tasted the sea and sail, knew of the freshness that it puts into a man's life and limbs. The motion of a heeling ship under billowing canvas had fascinated me from boyhood days, like a disease which I could not get rid of. Small wonder that I chafed and cursed in the mustiness of a journalistic life.

But in those two years I had skimped and saved that I might buy a little vessel like the *Thelma*. Now that I had got her I needed money enough to fit her out and break the last bonds which held me to drudgery and convention, the life of the herd in that stinking city.

With Bully things were different. His ponderous physique reflected his character. A mighty impassiveness allowed him no excitement or emotion. An engineer turned policeman for lack of something better to do, he trudged through life just as he trudged round his beat, unaffected by the whirl of traffic, the cries of the costers and jostling, motley crowd about him.

Eagerly I watch his face as I unfolded my plans. He did not look interested: sometimes I thought he wasn't listening.

"Well," I said at last, "there's the idea. It's up to you to decide. If we go we'll just have to take things rough and tumble and let tomorrow look after itself."

Bully yawned and looked at the bar clock.

"Come on. Let's go home and go to bed. They'll be chucking us out in a few minutes."

"But what about the cruise? What do you think of it?"

"Oh yes. Good idea. I'll come."

And thus the "great adventure" was decided upon.

We settled down to become misers and skinflints. In spite of an occasional lapse, we saved consistently; but it was a long and dreary business. We let a third party into our secret; one Dick Crowhurst, but he was too concerned with home ties to entertain the idea of accompanying us. Nevertheless, he helped us get the boat ready and often came down the river with us, or round about the Thames Estuary when we were sail stretching or drilling ourselves in the routine which would be necessary on a long passage.

After twelve months the saving business did not look very encouraging, but we snatched three weeks' holiday for a run down-channel. This was not in the nature of another test for *Thelma*, for it proved to be a fine-weather trip, and only served to give us moral refreshment to proceed with our plans.

Gradually the necessary equipment was got together. New sails, new water tanks, rope, wire rigging, charts. The cabin was enlarged to accommodate a galley aft, so that we would not have to cook in the forecastle, which was an impossibility in heavy weather such as we had experienced on that passage home from Emden in 1931.

At last I felt that the finances justified putting *Thelma* in a shipyard at Whitstable. The shipwrights sheathed her with Muntz metal, gave her new keel bolts and extra fastenings. Bully and I took her upriver to Erith to complete the fitting ourselves. In our every spare moment we were cleaning ballast, scraping bilges, making new rigging, painting, varnishing and wondering if ever we should be ready for sea at all.

We decided that we should not. If we did everything to the boat we wanted to do we should spend a lifetime labouring there on Erith marshes. So the first big step was taken.

Resignation day.

Our respective employers concealed their feelings with marked restraint. When I faced the Editor-in-Chief of the *Daily Mail* in his holy of holies he told me that we shouldn't even get across the Bay of Biscay. Others of the journalistic world expressed themselves in more voluble and less complimentary terms.

Metropolitan P.C. 356 reported "all correct, sergeant," on the last day of March 1934, and is alleged to have booted his helmet round the station yard on coming off duty. Rumour has it that he kissed the cook and made a rude sign at the photograph of the All Highest Police Commissioner hanging on the mess room wall.

We met in London on a night to be remembered and held a party with a few wicked friends. We fought our way out in the early hours of the morning and, with our dunnage bags on our backs, made our way down to where the *Thelma* lay to her moorings at Erith. Only Dick Crowhurst came to see us off.

A leaky punt lay alongside a rickety causeway which had been built some years before by some enthusiastic yachtsmen. It presented a constant danger to life and limb, but we successfully negotiated it (no mean feat in the circumstances) and Dick rowed us aboard.

The morning broke dull and chilly, with a south-easterly breeze blowing over the marshes. We pulled on our guernseys and pea jackets. Somehow we couldn't believe that we were really starting, going away for an indefinite period. We couldn't believe that we might not see Dick again for many a long year. But it was so.

In silence the mainsail was hoisted and the jib set up in stops. Dick went forward as I took the tiller.

"Cast off!"

Splash! Over went the mooring buoy. *Thelma* swung gracefully on her keel and glided downstream on the swiftly ebbing tide.

Dick remained on board until we approached the first bend in the river.

"Well. Good-bye, you chaps."

We shook hands all round and without another word he jumped into the dinghy, cast her loose and rowed back to the causeway. As we rounded the point I looked back and saw his tall, straight figure standing on the shore looking after us. His heart, I knew, was aching to be with us, but the fates ruled otherwise. Our only regret was that we had to leave him behind.

Our departure was just as we would have had it. No family farewells and weeping females. No waving handkerchiefs from the shore. Just "Good-bye, Dick," and that was all.

So down through the daily pageant of London River, tack and tack with big sailing barges, dodging between cargo steamers, lines of lighters, tugs and the multitudinous craft which crowd the lower reaches.

We spent the night in Hole Haven creek, a narrow strip of sheltered water on the Essex side of the Thames Estuary. Thence down to the Isle of Sheppey and Harty Ferry, there to retrieve two anchors we had been forced to leave at the bottom of the River Swale some three months before.

After playing the interesting game of "odd man pays" with some sailing barge skippers in the Ferry House Inn we went aboard to prepare for the open sea. Apart from the usual deck work this meant stowing all our food and belongings in places where they would not be disturbed- by the pitching and rolling of the boat. This task does not consist of sitting on the edge of a

bunk and thinking out nice handy places to put things in. It
means crawling about on hands and knees: jamming tins of food
in all sorts of quaint little nooks and corners; wriggling on one's
belly round the forecastle floor knocking in wedges with a
sixpenny hammer (the head of which flew off at the slightest
provocation) and generally performing strange contortions
entirely unnatural to mankind.

All the time we were thus engaged the wind was piping up
steadily from the north-east and by seven o'clock in the evening
was of sufficient strength to warrant an excuse to delay going to
sea until the morrow. But we argued that if we were prepared to
undergo any hardships which came our way it would be a poor
start to demur about putting to sea on a windy night. Thus, in
spite of the foreboding prediction of the skies, it was "up stick
and out of it" as the old seamen used to say, and *Thelma* was
hauled on the wind as we cleared the dangerous shoals off
Whitstable.

Neither of us slept that night, and when the dawn broke we
were heeling to a north-easterly gale. It was wet and cold, but we
had the consolation of knowing that we had a following wind to
take us down-channel. The prevalent winds in the English
Channel are from south-west and west, and for a sailing vessel,
unaided as we were by any mechanical power, it is generally a
long and tedious business tacking back and forth in that turbulent
stretch of water.

I had sailed down-channel many times before, but that
passage in the *Thelma* was the most uncomfortable I have ever
experienced. The wind shifted to the east and howled incessantly
as we tore along under close-reefed canvas. Steep following seas
bore down on us threateningly, and at last we were forced to pay
out long warps over each quarter to reduce the danger of being
pooped by a sea breaking over the stern. Two trailing warps help
considerably in smoothing down the dangerous whitecaps and
also, if the warps are long enough and heavy enough, they assist
the steersman in his task of keeping the vessel from broaching-to.

In a matter of a few hours we had acquired valuable but, at the
time, very depressing, information. Firstly, we learned that the
ancient and mouldy oilskins with which we were equipped were
quite inadequate for the purpose of keeping dry, or even warm.

Secondly, that our decks leaked deplorably and to lie in a bunk
was to be subjected to what Bully described as Chinese torture.
Drip — right on the forehead. Ten seconds interval. Drip — right
in the same place. Another ten seconds interval. And so it went
on until the would-be sleeper leapt out of his blankets in despair
and retired to the open cockpit where a continual drenching was
much more conducive to sleep than the Chinese business within.
Thirdly, we discovered that the so-called watertight box in which
we kept our supposedly dry clothes was not so watertight as we
imagined.

So generally speaking we didn't feel too happy. The only
thing that livened us up a bit was the fact that *Thelma* averaged
over seven knots from the South Foreland to St Catherine's
Head, Isle of Wight. She covered the distance in nineteen and a
half hours, and it was the fastest run she had ever made with us.

Just to show the tricks the sea can play with a man, we were
becalmed all the next morning in Poole Bay. Not a breath of
wind. Just a damnable swell left by the gale which sent our spars
a-crashing and the sails shaking. Not even our spinnaker, a sail of
exceedingly delicate texture, would draw.

But the warm sunshine dried our clothes and cheered our
drooping spirits. Internal needs were satisfied with hot beans and
tea. The blankets were brought out in the sun to steam.

And so to Poole when the breeze came.

The Bay and the Straits

In a cosy tavern by the waterside at Poole we sat before two foaming pints of ale. And when the tankards were empty we called for more ale, and maybe a hunk of bread and cheese to bear it company. Now and then we would rise to join in the ancient sport of darts, at which our lack of skill was frequently exposed by a trembling old fisherman of eighty-odd years of age.

Time to kill. We had nothing to do but watch and wait. For three days *Thelma* had been subjected to a thorough and final overhaul, and all except the work of the paintbrush had been completed. Our artistic efforts had been terminated by showers of rain, so we decided to put to sea at the first sign of a favourable wind.

For a week the wind blew steadily from the south-west and for the course we intended to take across the Bay of Biscay it was a dead nose-ender. So we just did our best to make the time pass as pleasantly as possible.

Thelma and ourselves provided the good folk of Poole with something of a mystery.

"They ain't fishermen," we could hear them say, "and they ain't yachtsmen. What's more, that there vessel b'ain't big enough to do no trading."

And as it was rumoured that *Thelma* was bound for "furrin parts" the mystery deepened and the waterfront of Poole either came to a secret solution or gave it up.

One night I was yarning with a fisherman on the quayside when I noticed that the wind had fallen light and tended to blow off the land instead of onshore as it had been all the week. I remarked about it to my companion.

"Ah," said he, casting his eye to windward, "them clouds have got some way on now. You'll 'ave a nor'west wind afore midnight."

A fisherman's word on the subject of weather is always to be respected, so I resolved that if the wind held nor'west all night it would probably do so for several days: whereas if it did not last till morning it would be of little use to us.

So we rose early the next morning and spat over the squaresail yard for luck. The breeze was still very light and we spent the morning doing odd jobs and having a final one over at the *Kings Arms*.

By midday the wind freshened and we took our mooring lines aboard.

"Let go aft!"

Thelma sheered across the narrow harbour, tacked and bore away for the open sea. This, I knew, was the last we should see of England for a long time — how long we could not tell. My last impression was of the one-legged ferryman resting on his oars and waving farewell in a sorrowful sort of way, as though he wished he was once more stumping round a ship's deck with an eagle eye on the billowing canvas aloft.

The Bay of Biscay is never a healthy place for a seaman, no matter whether he trusts his life to a fishing smack or a liner. Once round Ushant anything might happen. Sometimes it is as calm as a lake, but a few hours hard blow can make it like Hades with the lid off. The wind is nearly always from the west and south-west and the current tends to pin a vessel in the Bay of Biscay and drive her towards the shore.

My experience of deep-sea navigation in a vessel of *Thelma*'s size was precisely nil. Imagine my dismay, therefore, when I discovered on the fourth day out from Poole that we had left our Bay of Biscay charts ashore. It was bad enough shooting the sun because, apart from his disinclination to appear at all, the rolling of the vessel made the angle measurements more or less approximate. So with several days of unreliable sights and no chart on which to lay off our position and course the navigation was greatly influenced by that old-time sailor's method of "by guess and by God."

After Ushant the next chart we had was one of Cape Finisterre, some 380 miles away. This gave us no chance of running for a port should we sustain damage in heavy weather. We would just have to stick it out if it blew hard, and hope for the best if anything went amiss.

It was therefore somewhat ominous to see, after a short spell of fine weather, a mountainous swell come rolling in from the west. Each day the swell increased although the wind remained light, sometimes nothing more than a few puffs from the east. The sky was constantly overcast by great grey clouds.

Something was going to happen. Somewhere out in the Atlantic it was blowing mighty hard. Could we get south quick enough to escape it? The weather just taunted us. Our sails slatted in the calm, and fifty miles a day was considered a good run (With a good breeze *Thelma* would reel off 130 miles a day). Often we had to stow the mainsail because the breeze would not fill it and the boom would swing wildly back and forth over the deck. In such circumstances we could only use a little storm trysail which did not need any spars.

Slowly we rolled on our way, our eyes continually scanning the western horizon. Sometimes at night we would signal a steamer with a flash lamp to check our position but the fact that *Thelma* generally disappeared from sight in the trough of the swell made it practically impossible for either us or the steamship officers to read morse code.

Several ships, in daytime, would come off their courses to see what our saucy little tub was doing so far from land. Maybe they thought we were sailors adrift in a lifeboat. We would raise our caps in a dignified manner, hoist our red ensign and signal "Whatcher Cock" in the best London River fashion.

Once we saw a little Dutch motorship, the *Cornelia*, of Groningen, chugging her way northwards and rolling as much as we were. One could not but admire those Dutch seamen who, although carrying cargoes at cut rates, did not mind plying their trade in all weathers in the very smallest type of vessel. Frequently I have seen auxiliary ketches from the ports of Holland crossing the North Sea in wintertime with so little freeboard that it seemed as though their scuppers must always be awash. Those Hollanders will load their little ships down to their utmost limits, but the crew is often nothing more than a seagoing family. Father is the skipper. Mother is the cook, and is not averse to doing a trick at the wheel in moderate weather. The mate is generally the eldest son and the rest of the family do such work as their respective ages permit.

On the evening of our ninth day at sea we were making spun-yarn and chafing gear. In a rolling calm, chafe was one of our worst enemies. A new sheet or a new halliard would be chafed through in a day by the continual slat, slat, slat, unless parcelled with stout canvas and served with spun-yarn.

While we were thus engaged the wind, which had been blowing languidly from the north, shifted round to the south-west. The swell coming in from the Atlantic had become worse than ever, and it was obvious now that the storm was upon us.

As Bully took the helm for the first watch (8 p.m. to midnight) I asked him to call me at the first sign of a hard breeze.

Bully would never disturb my slumbers unnecessarily, but at eleven o'clock that night he blundered into the cabin and kicked me gently in the ribs.

"Bob."

No reply.

"Bob."

Still no reply.

"Bob!"

Hence the kick in the ribs.

I was dreaming that I having lunch with Gladys Cooper in a cosy Soho cafe and it was rather a rude awakening to be kicked in the ribs and find myself somewhere in the Bay of Biscay on a particularly black and stormy night.

It was so dark that, in spite of the smallness of our vessel, we could not see from one end of her to the other. The wind was beginning to whine in the hounds and some of the waves were capped with ugly white foam.

"Nice night," said Bully with a touch of sarcasm.

"Nice night be damned. What have you made so far this watch?"

"Twelve miles by log."

I stumbled below, for *Thelma*'s motion was becoming very violent, and grabbed the chart of Cape Finisterre to lay off our position by dead reckoning. To be certain of weathering the Cape we really needed more westing to allow for the inshore set, but to escape the storm our only chance was to work to the south before the weather became too bad.

I took over at midnight for the graveyard watch, and although I only got three hours of sleep that night I had plenty to do to prevent me from feeling drowsy. Carrying all the sail we dare, *Thelma* bucked and wallowed her way to the southward just as though she knew we were doing our best to save her from a severe dusting. Hour after hour she breasted the seas like the good old Cornish smack she was, and we felt that if only we did our part she would see us through.

And she did.

In the morning we found that we were out of the worst of the weather. The great black blotches in the sky were well down on the northern horizon. A brilliant sun gave me a good longitude sight and showed us to be thirty miles west of Cape Finisterre. We had run out of the storm and into the weather which one usually associates with the sunny coast of Spain. A smart northerly breeze sprang up. Little white tufts of cloud scudded overhead. Our first taste of the Portuguese Trades.

We looked astern and gave the Bay a salute. Biscay is Neptune's playground. It is here that he likes to work off his jokes and play merry hell with poor sailormen. After giving us a week of beautiful weather it was as if he suddenly woke up to the fact that he was letting us off too lightly. So it seemed that he roused himself and aimed a brick at the saucy little *Thelma*.

But she just bucked her stern and said, "Missed me!" — and carried us down to sunshine and safety.

The next night we made Cies Island, the sentinel of Vigo Bay, and after a brief calm we stormed through the North Channel in a series of violent rain squalls. So fiercely did the rain drive across the water that the land, close on each side, was completely blotted out. After nearly running down the French Fleet, which was anchored off the town, we tore on past the harbour and up to a quiet little spot called Ensenada de San Simon.

Here, sheltered on all sides, it was so still after eleven days at sea that I remember how peaceful it seemed to hear a cock crowing on some nearby farm. Our anchor down, we partook of a leisurely meal, our tranquillity being disturbed only by a boatload of swarthy caballeros and beautiful senoritas, clad in brilliant shawls, singing haunting Spanish songs with the accompaniment of a few guitars.

We spent a week in Vigo - town of ox-carts, sleep and sunshine. We learnt the meaning of mañana, and were only too willing to fall into Spanish ways and appreciate the art of doing nothing. Sometimes we would lean ungracefully on the quayside and watch the tourist ships come in, and see their assorted passengers fleeced by the ever-ready vendors who waited to welcome them on the landing steps. Sometimes, as the sun went down, we would repair to some cafe of ill repute, there to consume a bottle of wine and watch the Spanish damsels shake their limbs and roll their eyes after the manner of their national dances.

But even such days of ease do not hold one for long, and we put to sea again, expecting fine weather and fair breezes for the 300-mile run down the coast to Lisbon. Just to disillusion us the crew of the *Fantome II*, a handsome barque-rigged yacht, told us that they had never seen such weather as they had just come through on passage from Madeira, and warned us that a vessel of *Thelma*'s size would not live through it.

All the same, after one particularly hectic night ashore, we found it advisable to put to sea immediately. Having cleared the islands at the mouth of the bay, we caught the full force of a wind blowing hard from the north. To make an offing from the shore *Thelma* had to sail beam on to the sea and many were the drenchings of spray which descended over us as we reefed the mainsail and snugged everything down in anticipation of a rough passage.

We ran 135 miles the first day and it wasn't long before we were lying to our anchor in the River Tagus, enjoying the varied aromas arising from the Lisbon fish market.

A day and a half in Lisbon, watching the women outspit the men, and off to sea again for a glorious run down to Gibraltar. Fair breezes, a smooth sea and sunny days made us feel that at last we were finding solace for our years of bondage in the smoky northern city. I have never made a more pleasant passage. If we wished to alter course the wind would politely shift so as to remain favourable. It seemed that nothing could go wrong.

Under squaresail and main we bowled along at a steady four knots and as the sun went down on the second day out of Lisbon we entered the Straits of Gibraltar. Here the winds converge into a bottleneck and sometimes blow in screeching squalls. This was the end of our lazy sailing. A squall hit us at two o'clock in the morning and the squaresail boom snapped clean in half. I leapt from my bunk and scrambled forward, only to be crowned by the broken end of the spar. But a good sail is worth more than a crack on the nut, so while Bully kept *Thelma* on her course I cursed and struggled in a welter of flogging canvas until it was brought to the deck and stowed. The sail was only 170 square feet, yet it took me an hour to get the damn thing under control.

The mañana habit got us very badly in Gibraltar, and what with fraternising with sailors from the warships and bathing with the handsome wenches in Catalan Bay it took us two weeks to get under way again.

During this time we crossed over to Algeciras to see the famous bull-fighters of Seville. On a sunny Sunday afternoon six bulls were duly slaughtered and towed out by teams of horses to the blowing of trumpets and the jingling of bells. A cruel business, especially for the poor old hacks, who generally lost their entrails before the day's sport was done. The bull, of course, had a chance to make a fight of it, although he was on a loser from the time he came prancing out of the stable door. But the poor old hacks were merely led blindfold to the slaying.

The fighters are undoubtedly skilled and daring. They are trained on farms from boyhood days and stand high in the esteem of the Spanish public when they reach the top of their profession.

A Spanish companion attempted to explain to us the various moves and passes which we could not understand, but we were in a similar position to an Eskimo watching the Cup Final. One cannot criticise a game without understanding how it is played, and there is so much to know about bull-fighting properly to appreciate it that it is impossible to pass an opinion of any value by seeing a single afternoon's killing.

There are many different passes made by the fighters with their scarlet cloaks, but the main idea, as far as I could tell, is that when the bull charges, the toreador or matador (whichever he may be) steps aside but holds the cloak in the path of the animal so that he should not swerve towards the man. The cloak is whisked over the bull's horns, and often the fighter will give the great body a bump with his hip as it goes by. This final audacity on the part of the man was always wildly cheered by the crowd.

A dangerous-looking job is the one of sticking barbed darts into the bull's neck. The man who does this has no cloak to help him but holds a dart in each hand. He advances towards the bull, shouting and stamping to make him charge. It seems that the bull must get him but he nimbly jumps aside, rams home his darts, one each side, and then beats evens for one of the shelters at the edge of the arena. The bull holds six darts before the picadors come on the scene mounted on their poor old blindfolded hacks. One horse is pushed into position and the bull's attention attracted towards it.

By this time the bull, enraged by his quick-footed tormentors and maddened by the darts in his neck, is only too glad to take his revenge on the horse. He hits the hack with a terrific impact and tries to throw it. Tearing up the piece of "protective" padding, the great long horns gore into the horse's belly, entrails fall out on the sand, the tortured horse screams with pain, and Englishmen turn their heads and spit in disgust.

Meanwhile the rider, clinging somewhat unsteadily to his seat, jabs at the bull with a long lance and rips him open down the back, causing him to bleed profusely.

Another horse is brought and once more the ghastly business is enacted while the spectators stand up and shout with glee.

Then comes the matador. He is the big noise of the whole concern. He carries a dark red cape and a rapier. Apparently the weight of the cloth is an important technical point, as he has several to choose from and frequently discards one for another.

Before facing the bull he makes a courtly bow to the president of the fight and dedicates the kill to some dark-eyed senorita in the audience. He then places his montera on the ground, just for a bit of swank. The montera is a hair pad worn on the back of the head to keep the fighter's grey matter in the right place should be thrown backwards.

He makes a few artistic passes and strikes some graceful poses as the tired bull tries to wipe him off the face of the earth. Our neighbour explained that the matador has to manoeuvre the bull into a posture which leaves him with his front legs apart and his head down.

Poised on his toes, the matador levels his rapier while the crowd falls into a tense silence. The matador lunges at the vital spot just abaft the bull's head. To make this thrust the man must throw himself almost on the horns, and if the thrust is a good one the bull is paralysed and death is almost instantaneous.

For a good thrust and a quick kill the crowd roars its approval, but sometimes the matador has to call for a second rapier and try again. Once we saw the rapier come out below the bull's shoulder and the animal stumbled round the arena coughing up blood in pitiful distress. When he fell one of the minions of the troupe appeared with a dagger and ended his agony with a skilful stab.

So much for Spain's age-old pastime. We had seen enough of it—all its pleasantries and brutality; its glory and its shame.

A couple of days later, lying off the old Waterport of Gibraltar, we awoke at four o'clock in the morning and decided to go to sea. We could not have picked a worse time. A westerly gale was blowing in the Straits and we tried to beat out against it with the current running at nearly three knots in the wrong direction. Perhaps we were mad to attempt it, but we banked our

chances on an ancient pilot book which told of a favourable
current close to the African shore.

We accordingly sailed across towards the towering cliffs of
Morocco and, holding a full mainsail, tried to work westwards
with the help of the pilot book's alleged current. Time after time
we tacked back and forth, drenched with spray and shivering
cold in spite of the torrid temperature ashore. It was damned hard
work. That is the only way I can describe it. And by midday,
after six hours of it, we had made but a mile of progress. By then
we had said enough about the pilot book to make the pilot turn in
his grave.

Disregarding the instructions, we tried to find ways and
means of our own of getting out of the Straits, which seemed
likely to imprison us indefinitely. But we fared worse than the
pilot book, for we were nearly carried by the current round the
wrong side of Gibraltar Rock, and it took us another two hours to
get back to where we had been at four o'clock in the morning.

With one despairing effort we stood right into Gibraltar Bay
and by eight o'clock in the evening arrived at a pleasant
anchorage known as Getares Bay, on the Spanish coast. Here we
brought up for the night, our twelve hours' buffeting having
resulted in a gain of seven miles.

The next day the wind blew harder than ever and, profiting by
experience, we stayed put and spent the day eating large
quantities of hot porridge, a favourite dish of ours in all climes.

At last the wind eased and we, arising at the unearthly hour of
3.45 a.m. to catch the tide, proceeded to make slow but steady
progress towards Tarifa. With the breeze a point further north,
which was to our advantage, everything looked rosy. The tide,
the influence of which can only be felt close inshore, served us
until half-past ten so that we managed to scramble up to a berth
off Tarifa after covering ten miles in six and a half hours.

The tide served again in the afternoon and, encouraged by our
success in the morning, we weighed anchor in great hopes of
clearing the Straits before dusk. Did we Hell! Tack and tack,
sheet home and keep her full. But it was no good. After three
hours we were lucky to get back to Tarifa harbour without losing
ground.

In the morning we set sail in a very different frame of mind. Bully wanted to know how long it would take to sail round Africa and come out on the other side of the Gibraltar Straits. I thought it would take about a couple of years and then he wanted to know how long it was since the last east wind blew in these parts.

However, we were in for a pleasant surprise. A fluky slant of wind enabled us to round Tarifa Point on the starboard tack so that we could lay away up the coast in fine style. It was too good to last. In the afternoon the breeze gradually fell away and left us becalmed, so that the best we could do was struggle across the Straits to Tangier Bay, there to pick up the evening tide.

As dusk came we were left without a breath of wind in water too deep to anchor. So out sweep and pull, my Bully boy, pull. And pull he did.

Bully worked hard that night. One by one he threw off his garments until, stripped to his birthday suit, he looked like one of the galley slaves of history as sweat ran down over his eyes.

Refusing to let me leave the helm to give him some relief, he propelled *Thelma* seven miles in seven hours by means of thirteen stone of brawn and muscle. As the result of his herculean efforts we arrived off Tangier at two o'clock in the morning and he didn't even demand a drink. Just a bowl of porridge.

By this time we felt that the Straits of Gibraltar demanded more than a moment's casual consideration. We had taken a dusting; we had been weather-bound; we had taken four days to make thirty miles. And there was still another seven miles to Cape Spartel.

We resolved to wait in Tangier for a Levanter, which is the local name for the boisterous east wind which sometimes blows in the Mediterranean. Often these Levanters blow with such force that considerable damage is done ashore. A great sea wall was being built at Tangier to protect the town against these onslaughts and at the same time afford shelter for shipping.

With time on our hands we decided to fill up our largest water tank, which held sixteen gallons. I was told that there was a well a couple of hundred yards from the waterside and we gaily borrowed a boat and rowed ashore with the tank.

Two hundred yards. No well. Another two hundred yards. Still no well. And so on we went until we had covered the best part of a mile.

We stood in a queue with donkey drivers, beggars and children all armed with pitchers and waiting their turn. We were eyed with suspicion and wonderment. There were some exclamations of impatience as we twirled the wooden disc which operated the pump, for it takes a lot of pitchers to fill a sixteen gallon tank.

At last we were topped up and overflowing, and manfully we heaved the tank down the pathway to the street. By that time our arms seemed to have stretched to twice their normal length and we were glad to dump our load round the corner and use it as a seat.

It was impossible. We could never carry it a mile over the loose sand to the seashore. We sat there in the road in a despondent frame of mind. The only solution was to empty out half the water and make a second journey, but Bully kept mumbling, "We'll get the bloody thing there somehow."

He got up and walked back to where the evil-smelling queue was waiting for water. Thinking he had gone to wet his whistle, for it was a very hot day, I took no notice of him until he suddenly reappeared leading a donkey.

Our ass was a small skinny animal which looked barely capable of carrying a loaf of bread, but we thought it would be worth while putting her to a trial of strength. The tank was hoisted on to her back and she took the weight without so much as the flicker of an eyelid.

"Now then," said Bully hopefully, "way-up, lass. Come on. Gee-up."

Nothing doing.

I tried the language I once learned on a farm in Kent.

Nothing doing. We slapped her quarters, dug her in the ribs and heaved at her bridle, but it was all to no good. A small crowd began to gather and snigger. Children laughed and called to us in Arabic.

Presently, having lost all hope of starting the ass by our own efforts and rapidly losing the little calmness and dignity we possessed, we returned to the well where we found her owner dozing on a stone seat, awaiting our return.

We woke him, but he did not speak English. I tried him with French but that was no good. Bully brought out a book entitled, "How to speak Spanish in a Fortnight", and began laboriously to read out, with a very English pronunciation, the phrases and verbs listed therein.

But the old Arab just scratched his beard and shook his head, so we took him by the arm and led him along to where Jemima was still standing patiently with our tank on her back. We demonstrated that something had gone wrong with her starting gear whereupon he roared with laughter until I thought he was going to throw a fit.

Having sufficiently recovered to stand upright, he produced from under his robes a long pointed stick with which he jabbed Jemima fiercely in the buttocks.

"Azi, azi," he cried, whereupon the ass moved off at a smart trot.

He handed us the stick and returned to his dozing place. Versed now in the secrets of donkey driving, we ran after Jemima and steered her with some difficulty in the right direction. Sometimes, with a lusty "azi" and an extra jab at her stern, we would get her going so fast that we were hard put to keep the pace. At other times she would slow down until we were in deadly fear of her stopping. But we got her down to the water and succeeded in relieving the lady of her load. Luckily the owner came down later on to fetch Jemima home, but he demanded ten francs compensation for the loan of her. This he indicated by showing us a Moroccan franc and holding up all his fingers. I held up one finger in reply, whereupon he made himself appear as though he were about to have an apoplectic fit.

This finger language went on for some time, to the accompaniment of much shaking of heads on both sides. Eventually we put three francs in his hand and he swung on to the ass's back and rode off mumbling and grumbling in his beard.

Anchored near *Thelma* was a 40-foot yacht named *Gypsy*, in which an Englishman and his daughter had crossed the Bay of Biscay in the month of January. This was an accomplishment to be proud of, especially as neither of them had ever been to sea before except as passengers in liners.

One night *Gypsy* nearly met her end. Her owner had put her ashore at high water so that he could have some Arabs scrub and paint her bottom. Just after midnight one of the rope stays which held her upright parted in the middle and she crashed down on her side on the hard sand.

In response to his call we tumbled out of our bunks and went to his assistance. All night we worked to save the plucky crew's possessions and prepared to haul the vessel into deep water on the next tide. Eventually we got her off with nothing worse than a severe strain. It was a narrow squeak for the yacht, but nevertheless the owner and his daughter lost many of their belongings. What had previously been a neat and tidy floating home was, in a matter of a few seconds, reduced to a hopeless shambles.

This Englishman was himself something of an adventurer. He had worked for a shilling a day as a navvy in the States, he had been a flying instructor in Egypt, been heaven-knows-what in England; and here he was crossing the Bay of Biscay in wintertime and planning to sail on to the eastern Mediterranean.

So between the *Gypsy*, Jemima and the bums ashore our days in Tangier were pretty well occupied, and we were quite unprepared when one morning the wind suddenly changed from west to east and a heavy swell came rolling into the bay.

It was the warning of a Levanter.

Fishing boats scurried to the anchorage and a large French yacht, the *Jacqueline*, came driving in and made such a landsman's job of bringing up that by the time her anchor was down she was nearly foul of us.

This Levanter was the wind we had been waiting for, so Bully hurried ashore in the *Gypsy*'s dinghy to beat the Arabs down in the market for some stores for our passage to the Canary Islands. For it was there we intended to go to pick up the north-east trades.

Meanwhile I loosed sails and within an hour we were flying down towards Cape Spartel and the open sea. That, thank God, was the last we saw of the Straits of Gibraltar!

To Tenerife

In olden days the Barbary coast had a bad name among sailormen. The place was lousy with pirates and the navigation was difficult. East of Gibraltar winds are fluky and unreliable. The difficulties with which a vessel is beset in Gibraltar Straits I have already recounted. And west of the Straits, round Cape Spartel and down the Atlantic seaboard, the land falls away almost to sea-level, making inshore sailing as dangerous as it is along the treacherous coast of Holland.

The pirates no longer range offshore but congregate in Tangier, there to snare the unwary in the more comfortable surroundings of cafes and dance halls. We were well rid of them and had survived the rigours of Gibraltar Straits. Now we were tackling the last stretch of this ill-famed shore on our way to the Canary Isles.

It was a good start, bowling round Spartel like *Britannia* in a breeze. For two days we lived on a sea of peace and contentment. With the wind on the quarter *Thelma* would keep her course with the helm lashed so that our methods of keeping watch grew to be lazy and unseamanlike. We would becket the helm a trifle to weather, carefully trim the sheets and select a comfortable place in the sun to give ourselves up to dozing and meditation.

We were even too indolent to consider the prospect of putting into Casablanca to see Alain Gerbault. We had been informed that the famous Frenchman was there making final preparations for his trip to the Marquesas Islands. So we bowed our apologies to Gerbault from thirty miles offshore and sailed on our way.

Sea roving was by now becoming ingrained in us, and life aboard *Thelma* began to take the shape of a routine. The man on the forenoon watch (8 a.m. to noon) would awaken, or rather be awakened, to find his breakfast cooked, and just before the meal I would take a sight of the sun for longitude while Bully jotted down chronometer time.

He who had been on watch since 4 a.m. would then turn in to make up a little sleep while the helmsman wracked his brains for ideas on dinner. When he came off watch at noon, at which time I had to get another sun sight for latitude, he would proceed to put his ideas into practice. Thus the unwelcome task of cooking was duly shared according to the watches, for whoever had the second dog watch below had to prepare the supper. And I might say that from time to time amazing and mysterious dishes were scraped off the bottom of the frying pan.

During our early days at sea, when stores were in plenty, we always had these three meals a day, with an occasional ship's biscuit to munch during the night watches.

Strange the things we used to talk about. Politics, sex, religion, psychology, history, war, marriage, disease -– any subject of which we had the very slightest knowledge. Often we would indulge in some solemn argument, putting forth the pros and cons of something about which, I suspect, neither of us had any knowledge at all.

I remember one time when we got very highbrow and commenced a joint criticism of Liszt's Hungarian Rhapsody, humming a bar or two, altering a note here and there and generally reorganising the whole tune. But the strain was too much for us and the conversation soon switched to more earthy matters.

One interesting pastime was to build an imaginary dream ship. She was to be a handy little topsail schooner manned by

Bully and myself and two of our closest friends. Every plank and timber was debated with weighty solemnity. Every spar and sail cut to the inch, and not a thought for expense.

Before we reached port we had completed a general idea of the whole of our dreamship and had begun to wonder if one day it would all come true and she would sail out of dreamland on to the seas of reality.

Once I called Bully out to see a shark, an uncommon sight in those waters. He was cruising back and forth in our wake, occasionally showing his great dorsal fin above the surface. But he did not come near enough for us to get a shot at him and we had no hooks big enough to try to catch him.

Soon we were to abandon our musings and drivellings, debates and discussions, for some more urgent occupation. We were not yet finished with the Barbary coast.

The pleasant northerly breeze freshened and shifted a couple of points to the eastward. Down came the mainsail and up storm trysail as the wind strengthened to a gale. Harder and harder it blew, and higher and higher rose the seas. For two days *Thelma* scudded before the weather without shipping a drop of solid water. Spray drove over her like a white mist and to open the cabin door meant wetting everything below.

On the second night things began to look pretty bad, but it was a fair wind and it seemed a pity to waste time by rounding up and heaving-to. So we took in the trysail and let the vessel bowl along under a flattened spitfire jib. The binnacle lamp would not keep alight, and we steered solely by the stars.

We paid out warps over each quarter and got up a can of oil from the bilge in case we should need to use it over the side.

In the morning there was little to encourage us. The sun shone brilliantly and the blue sky was prettily patterned with tufts of flying scud, but the gale continued to screech in the rigging. And all the time the barometer remained as high as in fine weather. It had not fallen a tenth from the time we had left the Straits. So, with no signs or symptoms to go by, we just ran on until the wind suddenly petered out in the matter of a couple of hours.

Down trysail; up mainsail. Becket the helm and away we go again with the man on watch doing nothing more than lie on the cabin top reflecting upon his lurid past.

Six days out of Tangier I reckoned we were nearing Tenerife, an island which boasts of a mountain peak some 12,000 feet in height and visible at phenomenal distances. I considered it unlikely that we should have any difficulty with our landfall. There was a view of it on the corner of our chart from a distance of sixty-five miles and steamship skippers had told me that it can often be seen from ninety miles. Well, if I couldn't make a landfall within ninety miles either way then it would be better for me to give up navigation altogether.

It was therefore somewhat disconcerting when Bully reported high land on the port bow just as dusk was closing. It was high land all right but not high enough for Tenerife. In fact there was nothing about it to suggest Tenerife. Moreover, my latitude sights, about which there could not be an error of any magnitude, did not show us to be yet so far south.

I began to fear for my longitude reckoning, and worked through the last few sights again—only to arrive at the same results.

We ran on for a time under square sail, but fearing we might run past Tenerife and be unable to beat back against the trade wind and strong Canary current, we hove-to to await daylight.

We were both very tired, so we turned in for a sound eight hours' sleep. Under trysail and jib *Thelma* was quite capable of looking after herself.

Dawn—no sign of land. We got way on her again and ran until noon. Still no sign of land. Yet according to my sights we should only be a few miles from the harbour of Santa Gruz de Tenerife.

By now I was casting a doubtful eye on our chronometer. Longitude sights of a star and the sun would not agree. The latitude sights, which did not require chronometer times, were certain to be correct and checked up accurately.

Thus I did not know whether we were east or west of Tenerife, and it remained for us to run along the latitude until we came to the island. But which way?

I suspected that we were east of the island, but if we ran west, and my surmise turned out to be wrong, we should be heading out into the Atlantic before a strong north-east trade wind with only a week's stores and no hope of doing other than run before the wind until we reached the American continent. It would be no use, in a 26-foot vessel, to try to beat back against a trade wind and a thirty-mile-a-day current.

The only way out of our dilemma was to sail along the latitude due east. If, then, we were west of Tenerife we would soon come upon it. Should we be to the east of it, as I believed we were, then we could do no worse than arrive off the coast of Africa, if we did not see any other islands of the Canary group on the way.

So east it was and, with a smart breeze and heavy seas abeam, we had to snug down to the very useful rig of trysail, fore and jib.

Soon we came upon the island of Fuerteventura, where it never rains for years on end. No wonder they breed camels there. Having identified this island and checked the distance we had run along the latitude, I found that at the time we turned east we could not have been more than a few miles from Tenerife. Yet there had been no sign of the 12,000-foot peak.

Turning our backs on Fuerteventura and its camels, we retraced our course and late in the afternoon sighted land ahead. It appeared to be a low rocky coast and nothing at all to indicate that it was Tenerife. Still clinging to my belief in the noon latitude sights, we stood on until close on dusk, when we were but three miles from the shore.

Suddenly it came upon me like the answer to a riddle. All that we could see was the lower portion of some gigantic cliffs. The whole of Tenerife was shrouded in a heavy mist which reached down to within 100 feet of the sea. We were looking underneath a curtain, and not until we came within hearing of the breakers did we see a towering range of mountains above us.

The lights of Santa Cruz blinked at us as the sun went down, and at ten o'clock that night we sailed into the harbour and found a berth in company with a line of lighters and an old Dutch dredger.

Next day I began to shake my head over the chronometer. The navigation on this particular passage had undoubtedly been a failure. And I was supposed to be the navigator!

With the suspected instrument under my arm I stepped aboard a Norwegian motor vessel, the *Daccomba*, and with mixed feelings found that we were 15 minutes and 56 seconds slow.

The rate of our wretched chronometer had, for some unknown reason, altered from three seconds a day to twenty-five seconds a day. No wonder the longitude sights went wrong.

The relief at finding myself absolved was tempered by the knowledge that we had an unreliable chronometer. This chronometer I had bought in London for nine pounds and it was intended to serve us for many years to come. And here we were, but three months out from home, and the damn thing less reliable than a shilling watch.

We had arrived at Tenerife at an unfortunate time. The dreamy, lazy island had awakened one morning to strikes and riots, bloodshed and gunfire. The British Consul advised us to make our stay as short as possible.

We were told by an Italian that a party of sprightly lads had seized the British Consul a few days before and requested him to say, "Long live the Republic." He said he had no objection to saying "Long live the Republic", and did so.

"Now," said the unwelcome visitors, "say, 'Die the Monarchy'."

At this stage of his story the old Italian chuckled and drew us out of the hearing of some loungers nearby.

"Mistère Consul, he make big wallop. Poncha de nose. Oh, I was there. I laugh, Funny. Oh, my God! Much blood. All men run." And the old chap nearly creased himself up with laughter.

So we acquired a certain respect for the British Consul.

The Spaniards were hospitable, and afforded us the use of the Club Nautica, off which *Thelma* was moored. In fact soon after we arrived we were invited to a dance. Thrilled at the thought of stepping the floor with the dark-eyed senoritas, we devoted ourselves to an inspection of our wardrobe.

We had each set out from England with a suit of clothes fit to go visiting ashore. Whom we thought of visiting I have no idea, but such mad thoughts do occasionally come into a failing mind. My natty blue serge had already been used as a pillow, a towel, a dish cloth and a lamp wiper, so I decided that for me dancing was out of the question. Bully, looking for his fashionable grey, eventually discovered a crumpled and evil smelling ball of something underneath the potatoes.

He sniffed at it suspiciously.

"This must be it."

And it was.

With no intention of breaking into the sanctity of the dance floor we paddled ashore in a couple of newly washed shirts and lined up at the bar kept by a friendly old German. This was soon to become the custom with us, but as the band struck up we were politely told that gentlemen in shirt sleeves must not remain in the club during these select functions. The German worded the message so well that we meekly repaired on board to play poker. That night I bet sevenpence and the Canary Islands against Bully's fourpence and the *King's Arms.* I lost. Bully took the sevenpence and told me what I could do with the Canary Islands, and Tenerife in particular. Somehow he seemed a bit disgruntled over the shirtsleeve affair.

Feeling a little out of place in the club in spite of the many good friends we met there, we set ourselves to the task of preparing for an Atlantic crossing. It had been our intention to go to the Cape Verde Islands and there wait until the West India hurricane season was over. It was a risky business to arrive in the West Indies between July and October, but hanging about the Cape Verdes for over two months didn't attract us in the slightest.

One morning we fished out the Atlantic chart and a grubby finger moved slowly up the South American coast.

"Now, if we could get south of the hurricane area and still hold the trades . ."

"What's this place? Oh, the Amazon River."

"Hmm. Too far south. No wind. Wait a minute. Hand me that india-rubber and let's see what this name is."

Some scratching and rubbing and two heads getting in each other's way.

"Georgetown."

That's how we came to make our decision. We would not wait for the hurricane season to pass. We would try to dodge round the danger area and slip into Georgetown. So I got a postcard and wrote home:

"Dear Mother. Have decided to make it a long weekend. Next address— do Poste Restante, Georgetown, British Guiana."

Next day we persuaded one of the locals to sell us some "painto blanco" and *Thelma* was canted over in deep water for a couple of coats on her topsides. While the paint was drying we overhauled our gear, cleaned the ship from top to bottom, ordered a new squaresail boom to replace the one which had broken at Gibraltar, and made out- a long list of stores required.

Life ashore did not interest us very much. The riots died down and there was not even a chance of a respectable up-and-a-downer.

None of the old stories of the islands seemed to be true. There were no giant dogs, as recorded in the logs of the ancient seafarers. The sacred distilling tree of Till, which was supposed to distil water from its leaves, did not even exist. There is a dragon tree at Tenerife, but not much like the one referred to in days gone by. The only point of interest was the fort near which we were anchored.

It was from this fort that the Spaniards had defended Tenerife from an attack by Nelson. Nelson landed on the mole, which is almost under the nose of the cannon, and made such an inviting target of himself that the Spanish gunners blew his arm off*. That was as long ago as 1797, but the Spanish soldiers are still very proud of the feat and told us the story over and over again.

The best thing about Tenerife is the people one meets there. Fair-haired, blue-eyed Germans, bluntly courteous in that strange, stiff way they have. Pale-faced Frenchmen, full of life and friendliness but, strange to say, disliked by nearly everyone. Bluff, red-faced Englishmen of the "retired on a pension" type, mostly living at Orotava, a small town on the north side of the island. Here and there a tall Scandinavian, always speaking perfect English. And, of course, the elegant Spaniard, outdoing all in graciousness and polish. Attired in the finest cut of English clothes, his slim dark figure presents a marked contrast among the northerners who have come to his climate to find the sun.

At first glance one would think that there were only two races of people living, or staying, in the Canary Islands — southerners and northerners. For what difference, except in manner of language, can one see between English, Germans and Scandinavians? And so little between Spaniards, French and Italians. Where there should only be two nations, there are six.

And homely folk wonder why war and pestilence are constantly hovering over their roofs. Too many boundaries, petty conceits and jealousies.

But all this is beside my story and is no more than the gist of some alcoholic arguments with a stranger at the bar.

Once a young Spaniard invited us to climb the 12,000 feet up Pico Teyd, but we were very thankful when the arrangements fell through. Fancy us climbing 12,000 feet! Bully was horrified.

Several times while we were refitting we were asked to take passengers. One swarthy soul said he would give us 50 pesetos and a sack of flour to take him to his wife and family in South America. He would work; yes, he had been a sailor, he said. "I sleep on deck," he added, in spite of our suggestion that he would probably have some damp and salty nights.

*In fact Nelson was shot in the right arm as he stepped ashore; the limb was later amputated by Thomas Eshelby, surgeon on board the *Theseus*, Nelson's flagship.

Another Spaniard, a stripling of barely seventeen years, desired a passage to Buenos Aires, and offered to bring his two handsome sisters. After deep consideration this overture was also rejected.

Best of all was a young French nurse who wished to accompany us for the purpose of supervising our general welfare. She could cook, she was a good nurse. She had no husband and no children.

"Vous parlez Français," she said, tapping me on the chest, "and for your friend here I speak a little English." And she had a catching laugh that nearly made me say, "Step aboard."

Bully was doubtful. He confided that the lady might become what he rudely termed a "bloody nuisance".

So we returned to our labours in order to get to sea as soon as possible lest we be subjected to further temptations.

At last all was ready. Stores were brought down and the water tanks filled. It was a gruelling job carrying water in the hot sun, so one of the small tanks, which had been filled up at Tangier and had not been touched, was allowed to remain. All the other water on board was changed for fresh and the Tangier tank was to be used first.

A local holiday delayed us and we met difficulty in buying paraffin for the lamps and primus. We were eventually directed to the musty establishment of a gentleman who was obviously a rogue. However, we needed paraffin and he sold it and said he could supply us with ten gallons. All the tins were filled except one. In spite of much draining and tipping of the barrel the last gallon would not drip. So our friend disappeared next door with the tin and reappeared with it full. Little did we suspect what he had topped the tin up with. The fates delayed the revelation until we were far away in the tumbling Atlantic.

The great day came. We bowed our thanks for the hospitality of the Spanish people. A young Englishman and his Norwegian lass came aboard with a bottle of Scottish ale. A German arrived with some München bier. There was a tin of something from an Anglo-Spaniard. Our pockets were stuffed with addresses we had promised to write to.

Soon, we glided out of the harbour. A light southerly wind carried us along the coast until evening. We turned westward towards the setting sun.

Tradewinds and Doldrums

Off the island of Hierro (which the ancients used as 0 degrees longitude because it was the most westerly known land) we streamed the patent log and settled down to the serious business of passage making; 2,800 miles of the Atlantic lay ahead of us before we should see land again.

No passage ever started with such evil forebodings. Just before leaving the Club Nautico a message was sent down to the effect that for the first time in history hurricanes had been raging along the north-eastern shore of South America — down Georgetown way.

The second day out we both fell ill. It was not sea-sickness, for three months' deep-water sailing in a 26-foot boat is long enough to bring the inner man to a state of complete submission. Bully lay on the cabin floor retching and coughing with a face like the day of judgement. For me it seemed as though some spirit had flown off with my legs. I could do no more than hang on to the coaming like a drunk in a daze. Slowly my knees sagged and wobbled until suddenly I sat down with a wallop on the cockpit floor.

I crawled to the galley and drank a mugful of water. Bully did the same. The result was that we felt even worse.

"That mainsail will have to come in," I said, feeling very dry and hoarse.

We hauled ourselves forward to the pin rail. Bully handed me the main halliard and went aft to steady the boom. There was a lumpy sea running and as I eased the peak the boom swung wildly in and hit Bully a terrific clump on the ear. Picking himself up he grabbed the rebel spar with what strength he had left and shouted to me to lower away. Down she came.

Just at that moment *Thelma*, having no one at the helm, lurched broadside to a breaking sea. There was a crash. I fetched up in the lee scuppers and heard Bully yelling for help. It seemed a long time before I could get back to the cockpit but I found the mainboom thrashing about in two pieces with Bully and the mainsail tangled up all round it.

We lashed it all down as best we could and let the vessel jog along under jib alone.

Bully stretched himself out on the cabin floor again. I sat lifeless in a heap at the bottom of the cockpit. *Thelma* looked after herself.

My throat was parched and burning and sweat poured off my body. I crawled to the water tank again. The water was cool and pleasant but produced a horrible feeling amidships. Bully took the mug from me and refilled it.

I seemed to doze off and when I awoke it was night-time. Stars were shining and *Thelma* was pitching along on a somewhat erratic westerly course.

I felt better, but thirsty. Bully was already awake and by the light of the cabin lamp sat regarding a small red insect in the palm of his hand.

"Where did you find that?"

"In the Tangier water. It's bad. Look at this."

He handed me a piece of linen through which he had strained some water. It held a reddish brown fungus. It was in this fungus that he had found the insect.

A pot of porridge made with water from another tank made us feel a good deal improved and we held a council of war.

We could not set the mainsail. There was no hope of fishing the boom because there was no deck space and the motion of the boat made it impossible to work. With a tankful of bad water we should have to be very careful with the rest and hope for a fast passage. There was no thought of turning back or running for the Gape Verde Islands, which would have been the most sensible thing to have done.

Full of hopes and hot porridge we set the squaresail and got *Thelma* on a west-by-south course. Away she went like a kicking horse, and all that day we surged along until the mighty peak of Tenerife sank from view in the evening.

By this time the crew had almost recovered, which was just as well, for a gale blew up out of the north and forced us to take in the squaresail and set a spitfire jib and storm trysail. Forced slightly off our course to ease the vessel, we kept her running. The night was as black as pitch.

I was at the helm for the graveyard watch when a big sea piled up on our quarter and struck us with such violence that I was thrown head first into the galley. Before I could scramble back *Thelma* broached-to and the next wave broke right over her, pitching high up in the trysail.

I shouted for Bully but he did not need any awakening. He was swamped out of his bunk and the cabin was already half full of water. He rushed out and grabbed the pump as I threw my weight on the tiller and held it hard up. There was water everywhere, and we could hardly tell whether the vessel was above the surface or below it.

I reached down through the water on the lee deck, found the trysail sheet, and let it fly. Bully hauled the jib aback with one hand as he pumped with the other. Only a man of phenomenal strength could have performed such a feat.

Slowly *Thelma* paid off, and when the next sea struck her she took it well abaft the beam and sluggishly rose to it.

Bully pumped while I steered and gradually *Thelma* shook herself free. In a quarter of an hour we had her bilges empty and Bully retired to a well-soaked bunk. It had been a narrow squeak.

The gale blew itself out in the morning and for a time our trials and tribulations were at an end. Day after day we ran before the trade wind under squaresail at the rate of over 100 miles from noon to noon.

The sun shone brilliantly; flying fish danced around us; deep-sea gulls swooped overhead; and in the evenings Venus and the Sun would sink down over the western horizon like a ball of fire and a shining jewel.

And such nights—the warm wind and sparkling sea; a multitude of stars such as we English folk never see at home. Trade wind life! I had read about it from my childhood days; pictured it in my dreams at home. This was it. All that I had expected. Everything I had hoped for.

At night the flying fish would leap at our port-hole light and land on the foredeck, so that all we had to do was to pick them up in the morning, gut them and drop them into a sizzling frying pan. These fish shoot out of the water by means of powerful strokes of their tails, and by spreading their wings in the manner of a gliding bird, manage to keep above the surface for distances of up to 200 yards or more.

Before our bow there swam a little striped pilot fish which had joined us just after we had passed Hierro. Day and night, at all speeds, he kept some eight or ten inches in front of the stem. We became so familiar with him that we named him Joe and looked upon him as ship's company.

I shall never forget those trade wind days. They were always full of interest. Schools of porpoises splashing merrily along would come off their course to leap around us after the manner of a friendly greeting before going on their way. We saw strange fish and an occasional whale; and once a great white bird hovered over us at a tremendous height. I have no idea what bird this was, as the albatross never comes north of the Line.

These wonderful days lasted for nearly a fortnight. We fed well and lived comfortably. Included in our stores was a stalk of about 240 green bananas which we had bought at Santa Gruz for five shillings. They were lashed up on the cabin to ripen on the voyage. We had not anticipated that they would all ripen at the same time, so that for three days there was such an orgy of banana eating that we could not look at anything else. Even so, the last sixteen went rotten and, to Bully's sorrow, had to be committed to the deep.

It was on our fifteenth day at sea that this sailing dream came to an end. The wind strengthened and after a few hours there was a heavy sea. We ran 122 miles that day, and I reckoned that we were half way across. I therefore took stock of our water and provisions and calculated that, if the potatoes did not go bad, we had enough to last us another thirty days. But we could not afford to be free with the drinking water, and consequently did not throw away the Tangier tankful in case it should be wanted in an emergency. At a pinch I thought we might strain and boil it.

The wind remained strong all night and the next day, gradually building up a huge following sea. *Thelma* ran at about six knots under the little squaresail.

It was at this point that we discovered that the salesman in the Canary Islands had put water in the paraffin to make up the quantity. The water made the Primus stove peter out just when things were about half cooked, which caused a stream of bad language.

It was not until the seventeenth day that the weather began to look really bad. There were violent rain squalls and heavy breaking seas. Driving cumulus came so low that it appeared to be only just above our masthead. The wind came dead out of the east and all the time the barometer fell steadily.

By midnight the wind changed from a steady gale to a series of terrific squalls and the sky became overcast by large black banks of cloud. I began to think in terms of hurricanes. Why had we not had the patience to wait for the proper season to cross the Atlantic?

Well, we were in for it, so we cast our regrets overboard and made the best of an ominous situation. After an earsplitting thunderstorm the wind eased up and in the morning there were occasional windless intervals. But all the time the rain came down in torrents and the sky looked as though the end of the world had come.

I altered course to south-west in case a hurricane was upon us, and hoped that by working further south we would get out of its path. Of course, there was the risk of running into it, but there was less likelihood of hurricane weather nearer the doldrums.

All that day and the next night *Thelma* heaved on a sea which seemed to threaten us with every pitch and roll. At night—more thunderstorms; and lightning so fierce that we dare not hold the iron tiller with a bare hand. Both of us sustained mild shocks from it, and took the precaution of steering with a piece of rope on the tiller head.

The rain helped to subdue the sea, and in the forenoon of the nineteenth day the wind began to blow in fitful gusts from the north-west. We set the trysail, fore and jib. Soon it was blowing hard again and the jib had to come in. I called Bully who was taking a nap below. In such weather I could not leave the helm.

He squeezed his massive shoulders through the hatch just in time to catch a solid lump of water in the back of the neck. He cursed and shook himself like a great dog. Casting his eye round the horizon he expressed himself in that one word which means so much to a Londoner.

"Blimey."

It was a devilish task, but Bully went forward and tackled it like a seasoned hand. Sometimes he had to lie on his back with his feet jammed in the lee rail to prevent himself being carried overboard. An old saying at sea is one hand for the ship and one for yourself, but this job was a two-handed one.

I shall never forget those trade wind days.

How Bully kept himself out of the Atlantic Ocean I do not know. There was the sound of blasphemy, a flogging and banging of canvas—and the sail was in. Bully came aft with an ugly weal rising on the side of his face—the mark of a flying rope end. I breathed a sigh of relief to see him safe.

"Anything else?" he asked calmly, as though we were yachting in the Solent.

"That's all, cock."

He grinned and clambered into the galley to set about peeling potatoes for dinner. He was enjoying himself, and his calmness and placidity in a tight corner was a blessing. And this was his first real trip to sea! All he had done before was an occasional weekend or summer holiday jaunt.

Another day's blow; and all through the night the wind shifted steadily in a westerly direction until at 4 a.m. it was due west and I was convinced that a hurricane was upon us.

Years ago, with my childish head full of ships and the sea, I had learned the seaman's rules for revolving storms. Little did I think that I would ever have to put them into practice. I repeated them to myself as I stood on watch in the early hours of the morning.

More blistering language and the trysail was lowered and stowed below. The foresail came down soon after and *Thelma* tore along under her bare pole.

I reckoned that we were on the edge of the left-hand semi-circle of the hurricane, and by keeping the wind on the starboard quarter we stood a good chance of getting out of the path of the vortex. Our object was to get behind the centre of the storm, which was travelling north-west. The seas were very confused and did not come from any particular direction. They were more like pyramids of water, from the tops of which blew a blinding sheet of spray. All through the day and night we were blown first to the south and then to the east.

Just before dawn on the twentieth day I noticed that the barometer had ceased to fall. The wind was then howling like a horde of fiends from the south-south-west and it was evident that we had escaped from the path of the storm and run round in a large semi-circle to the rear of it.

The hurricane was now moving away from us and we laid out our sea-anchor on a long stout warp. But the sea-anchor was of no help to us. We found afterwards that the canvas, although sewn to an iron hoop and strengthened by wire rope, had been torn to ribbons by the weight of the vessel dragging it through the water. In any case it was impossible to ride head to sea, for it came in all directions.

The best *Thelma* could do was sheer about from six points off the wind to about one point abaft the beam. Everything was lashed down, even the coils of rope on the pin rails. The fore-hatch had long been bolted and caulked and the galley hatch was drawn over until only a crack remained to ventilate the cabin. The tiller was lashed amidships and the broken pieces of boom were wedged and lashed in the scuppers so that Hercules himself could not have shifted them.

We could do nothing more. *Thelma* must struggle for her own existence - and ours. Our lives were in her hands.

To occupy ourselves and our minds, we jammed ourselves in on the cabin floor and commenced a long game of cards. During the course of the day I lost four and sixpence, a pair of seaboots and a canvas shirt. Had the hurricane lasted another day I should have had to go on watch in the nude.

After midday we noticed the wind to be easing and blowing in squalls and gusts, with occasional lulls. It was nearly over. At four in the afternoon we set the storm trysail and the spitfire jib to steady her violent motion. She bore the canvas well enough and began to edge her way to the north-west.

The storm had past.

The next day the swell persisted without a breath of wind, but towards evening a light north-easterly breeze sprang up and once more we jogged on our way westward. By the next noon we had run fifty-one miles and all was well.

Trade wind weather again. But we had been driven too far south to hold it. The breeze was fitful and although one day we did 120 miles our runs diminished too rapidly for us to get back on our proper course.

On the twenty-seventh day it fell dead calm. *Thelma* lay on a glassy sea, gently heaving on an oily swell. Above us tufts of white cloud sped across the sky, yet we could not feel a breath of wind. We were in the grip of the dreaded doldrums.

Two courses were open to us. Either to steer north towards the West Indies to pick up the edge of the trades again or to work our way to the southward to find the south-easterly wind which blows up the South American coast from Cape San Roque.

We were not given an opportunity to decide, because without a breeze we could not do anything: and without a mainboom we could not make much progress against a headwind. The next day was the same — and the day after. I read an ancient sea story which referred to a ship finding a breeze in these parts some 400 years before. That must have been the last one.

After the first four days of the calm I began to feel uneasy, and carefully tallied our stores and water. Many of the potatoes had gone bad, but the water was the principal problem. We had set out from Tenerife with sixty-five gallons and there were only twelve gallons left, in addition to the Tangier water. It was insufferably hot, for the sun was almost ninety degrees at noon.

We rationed ourselves to half a pint a day each. Little enough in tropical weather. It meant no more than three sips between daybreak and dusk.

There was no telling how long it would be before we got a breeze, and it was 360 miles to the nearest point of land— the coast of French Guiana. To get there we had to cross the doldrums. There would be much less likelihood of a continued calm if we could get north to the trades, but the total distance to land would be much greater and through the hurricane area.

Another day of calm and we began to get thirsty—very thirsty. It was not so much the actual need of water as the tantalising knowledge that it was there in front of us but must not be touched.

By the seventh day of the calm our interest in this world was limited almost entirely to water. We began to get hoarse and talked little; dry lips, cracking and full of salt. Now and then, in the heat of the middle day, we would take a sip of the strained and boiled Tangier vintage.

As we were watching the sun come up on the eighth day (our thirty-first day at sea) I suddenly remembered that there were four bottles of beer in the bilge. Beer! Think of what it meant to us stuck out there on a windless ocean on half a pint of water a day!

It took less than ten seconds for those bottles of beer to be ranged side by side on the cabin floor. I eased the stopper off the first one with a trembling hand. In a moment I was smothered in a welter of foam. The stopper blew off and when I looked into the bottle there was not a drop there.

Bully tried the next one and was more successful, but no sooner did we take a mouthful each than we rushed to the rail and vomited in an appalling fashion. The intense heat had turned the beer bad.

The next night I tried lowering the two other bottles over the side on a long line in the hope that the cooler water further down would put them to rights, but it was no use. The stuff had a stench so nauseating that we had no compunction about slinging the bottles and their contents overboard.

Soon we were to have visitors. A small shark appeared and swam lazily round the boat. It was not long before he was joined by others, and they got so saucy as to make a lunge at the dinner plates as we washed them over the side.

That was enough. War was declared. We had no shark hooks and no bait but, armed with a coal hammer, a knife and a large marlinespike Bully and I would man the rail and wait for one to break surface. We would then belabour him with great gusto before he had a chance to dive. Of course, we had not the slightest intention of catching one, but it kept our minds off the water problem.

Sometimes I would fish with a small hook and a piece of potato peel with remarkable success. Foolish little fellows with yellow tails (about the size of a pilchard) would grab at my bait, and half a dozen of them would make a good meal with a couple of potatoes. Unfortunately we could not rely on them. One day I would get a dozen or more of them and another none at all.

This being so, we carefully counted over our potatoes and the reserve tins of lamb's tongue. We had brought sixty tins from England, and by this time the sight of it was far from appetising. Made into soup, fried with mashed potatoes or stone cold from the tin, it was lamb's tongue just the same.

It was necessary to cut down to one meal a day, consisting of half a tin of tongue each and two potatoes. When fishing was good the tongue was saved.

We found that by eating less we did not feel so much the craving for water; although there was nothing we would have liked better than a square meal and a gallon of ale, we felt better for our restricted diet.

Once or twice there came a languid air which would give us a mile or so to the north and north-west. But this barely affected us, as my sights showed that we often drifted as much as twenty miles a day to the south and east — the wrong direction, of course.

Once I came on deck and found that Bully had rigged a jigger sail by setting the reaching foresail from the topping lift to a bumpkin consisting of a

We found that by eating less we did not feel so much the craving for water.

long sweep lashed to the taffrail. While the gust lasted this arrangement was quite successful.

During these days of deathly stillness we did our best to keep occupied without expending any energy liable to work up a thirst or an appetite. We wrote letters, read books and made little ornamental oddments out of rope and canvas. So far as the books were concerned we had a somewhat feminine selection. While at

Tangier, we had swapped libraries with the girl in the *Gypsy*. She got a sackful of sea stories, Wild West magazines and various periodicals which a respectable man would hesitate to take home. In return we got a stock of lovelorn tales, of heart-broken maidens and handsome men in Monte Carlo. Just the things one would expect a girl to read. But we were not in a position to pick and choose, and read them all over again.

One particularly well read journal was an old London evening paper which we found serving as a shelf cover in the food locker. We learnt the race programmes by heart, memorised the houses to let, and read the news columns more times than any editor could ever dream of a reader doing.

A morbid occupation was the compilation of a death list. Assuming that we would not see England again for another three years, we jotted down the people we expected to find dead on our return. Age, state of health, recent illnesses and the possibilities of a weak heart were all taken into consideration, and it took us a week to get together a list of eight.

Ten days calm. Food and water were getting very low. The sky was a sheet of blue with an occasional wisp of white.

Ravenous as a pair of wolves, we fished with feverish anxiety and the patience of Job, but our luck was out. Not a bite for three days. Only sharks cruising round and round like dogs waiting for scraps from the table.

Midday. The sun beat down mercilessly on our naked bodies. It was stifling hot in the shade of the cabin and scorching in the sun outside. The best we could do was to stretch out on the cabin floor and try to sleep. Sleep, when we could, was at first a cure for all our ills. One does not feet hungry and thirsty when in the land of dreams. But soon we came to be dreaming of cooling fountains and gushing waterfalls, and that made things all the worse on awakening, so we gave up steeping except at night and started going through the library again.

The tenth day was a memorable one. Late in the afternoon a long black cloud, like a huge sausage, rose in the south. It seemed to spread down to the sea. Rapidly it came towards us—a rainsquall!

We hurriedly got out a tarpaulin and spread it on the cabin top. Plates, dishes, saucepans, anything that would catch water, were set round the decks.

Then the squall missed us.

Thank heavens, our disappointment was not for long. More squalls came up, this time from the westward, and soon there came one which could not possibly miss us.

The rain beat down and stung our sun-scorched bodies. We drank greedily at first, but soon restrained ourselves lest we did ourselves harm. Six gallons we stowed away in the starboard tank after that squall had passed, and in the breeze that accompanied it *Thelma* pushed her way some three miles to the north-west.

We felt like lions at the kill. More squalls. More rain. More wind. As Bully caught water I cracked on the squaresail and set the trysail as a studdingsail.

It was calm again at night, but next day we picked up a moderate north-easterly wind which occasionally blew in violent squalls. We were on the edge of the trades again.

The sun had opened up our decks and they leaked like a basket. The spray and rain gave us no peace below, and although we made a run of eighty miles by the next noon we were both dog tired. There was no sleep for us. While the wind lasted we had to make the most of it. For three days we drove on with the wind gradually falling away until at last we were again left in a still, oily calm.

For the next three days there was not enough breeze to blow out a match. The water ration, which had been increased to a pint after the rain, was again cut down, and we decided to chance our luck with the next wind and head straight across the western end of the doldrums for the Guiana coast.

On the night of the third day of this second calm (our forty-first day at sea) a light air came from the east and we shaped our new course with our hearts in our mouths. If we did not quickly reach the region of the south-east wind we might easily have another month at sea. Two weeks would put us down to half a dozen potatoes and a couple of tins of lamb's tongues.

It was hell or Georgetown, so we laid west-south-west and set everything. The day's run was marked off each noon with pedantic precision. Thirty-two miles. Sixty-seven miles. Another dawn and the wind shifted to the south-east. Quickly it strengthened until it blew so smartly that a sea began to kick up around us, and flying fish once more flitted along the waves.

It was like old times again. The helmsman would sing aloud with sheer delight. The very sea gave us life and spirit. We were in the wind track again. All was well.

One hundred miles. Eighty miles. The daily runs were read regularly, and *Thelma* fussed her way along like an old lady in a hurry. The seas came shorter and steeper. The water looked green instead of blue. We were nearing land.

On the evening of the forty-sixth day I was convinced we were over the shallows which stretch for many miles off the coast of Guiana. We sounded. No bottom at twenty fathoms.

I took a set of three sights and from the resultant position we laid bets as to when we should see the land. I made an optimistic entry in the log — "expect to make the land early tomorrow."

At 4.30 in the morning I thought I saw a glimmer off the starboard bow. A steamer went by, but the glimmer remained. Just before dawn broke it took the form of two flashing lights. Daylight came too quickly for us to identify them, but if they were not the lights of Georgetown, as I believed them to be, then they indicated Surinam (Dutch Guiana).

It seemed too good to be true that we had hit Georgetown dead ahead. Rations were trebled and I was in the galley cooking breakfast (flour and water, fried in olive oil) when Bully called me out.

Fluttering above us was a beautiful white butterfly. We sounded again and found sixteen fathoms and a muddy bottom. We made the land at noon. From the masthead I could see the smoking chimney-stacks of the sugar factories, tall, swaying palms and neat little white houses dotted along the shore.

It was characteristic of Bully that he did not even trouble to turn out of his bunk to see the welcome sight until it was time for him to come on watch.

Hospitable Georgetown

"Is it Demerara?"

Bully pulled on a pair of tattered and totally inadequate pants and spat gracefully over the side.

"Yes. Georgetown must be a bit to starboard."

"What's that contraption over there?"

I trained an ancient pair of binoculars upon the object he pointed out to the north-west.

"Dunno."

"Isn't it the Demerara beacon?"

"May be."

"Betcha."

He was right. The great beacon, standing nine miles offshore, came rapidly into view as we sailed peacefully towards the land. The beacon marked the channel into Georgetown.

All that afternoon the breeze was light and flukey, sometimes leaving us in a flat calm. Close inshore there passed a four-masted schooner; an ugly, slab-sided thing in spite of her nicely fitting canvas. Now and then steamers appeared and sank from view over the horizon astern of us, bound to the southward from the States. Strange birds circled overhead and flew back to the land as if to take tidings of our coming. An aeroplane hummed across the sky.

After our lonely days at sea all these things seemed so homely, such friendly and welcoming sights. And the land so near — we could hardly believe it was not all a dream. I expected to wake to the familiar "Watch-O" and find myself still in the midst of that wild waste of water.

So light was the wind that it was evening before we reached the beacon and, having no chart of the entrance to the Demerara River, considered it advisable to wait until daylight. What was one more day after forty-nine days at sea?~

So we jilled around near the light, but just to celebrate the last night of our passage we had a rough and tumble with squalls, rain and thunder storms. To hold our position near the beacon when there was very little wind we had set a big light-weather jib. Without warning we were struck by so hard a squall that the jib had to come in with the vessel heeling over at a perilous angle.

Before I could get to the outhaul and halliard the sail carried away in the head and I did not improve it by getting it caught up in the bitts as I muzzled it down in a hurry.

That was the only sail damaged during the whole passage from Tenerife, and I must say that it was an old one and not made of heavy flax like the rest.

Morning came without a breath of wind. No sooner was the sun above the horizon than there came a stifling heat.

I saw a huge negro standing on the staging which surrounded the beacon. Silhouetted against the rising sun he seemed like a great giant. He was the first human being we had seen for fifty days and we gave him a lusty hail. He shouted back and made some signals which we did not understand.

Presently some more men appeared from the door of a wooden shelter and gazed at us for some moments before manning a motor launch which lay alongside. In a few minutes they were rounding up on our quarter.

"Catch the line, mister."

We caught the line and were towed to the staging and made fast. The huge man we had first seen gazed down on us from the top of the ladder with an air of curiosity.

"Come right up. Where've you come from?"

We shook hands and I explained who we were and how we came to be there. He listened politely but, I thought, a little dubiously.

"Well, come and have a cup of green tea. Boy—get tea."

We sat in a little anteroom and drank some of the most welcome tea I have ever tasted. The negro, who turned out to be a pilot, told us of the times he had been to England as a soldier in the Great War. Taking us outside, he pointed out the landmarks for negotiating the tortuous channel over the shoals to Georgetown.

"Here in Georgetown is a good place," he said. "Not too much work. No one starves."

By now a breeze had sprung up from the south-east and, bidding our host and his comrades farewell, we set forth for the mouth of the river. We did not know that while he had held us in conversation the beacon wireless operator had sent a message to the shore to the effect that two escaped convicts from Devil's Island were making for the port.

Apparently many convicts from the ill-famed French settlement escaped in small boats and made their way up the coast, often getting as far as the Dutch West Indies and Venezuela. Port authorities would not harbour them, but generally gave them stores and sent them on.

It was quite excusable, therefore, that the negroes on the beacon, seeing a pair of half-naked, bearded savages in a small boat, should have taken us for late residents of Cayenne. The story of our coming from England was too fantastic for them to believe.

Bully took her in while I straightened up the ship and tried in vain to make everything look neat and tidy. While below I found the remains of a broken mirror. Out of sheer vanity I looked in it.

There I saw a sun-scorched face, largely covered by a long beard. Not a respectable beard such as old men wear at home but a wild, bushy, luxuriant affair, with a moustache and hair over the ears. With a patch over one eye, which had been slightly injured, I barely recognised the reflection. I quizzed at Bully through the cabin door as he stood at the tiller working the vessel from buoy to buoy. His usually pale face had turned olive brown. His hair hung down the back of his neck like an ill-fitting wig. His beard had grown after the fashion of a seventeenth-century aristocrat. Short and pointed, with a little tuft under the lower lip, he looked like a figure stepped out of a history book.

I threw the piece of looking glass overboard lest I frighten myself, and went out to respond to the hail from the customs launch which had come out to meet us.

The boarding officer was one of those cynical, damnably efficient young men who didn't care whether we had come from heaven or hell provided we had the necessary papers; and in this respect he appeared to be gravely suspicious. He glanced at our Tenerife Bill of Health and sniffed. "Got any more?"

I gave him one from Gibraltar and he scanned it with a very critical eye. "You say you've come from England?"

"Port of Poole."

"Then where's your Poole clearance?"

By this time, now knowing the reason for his suspicions, I began to feel rude. "Here," I said gruffly, handing him a bundle containing five Bills of Health, passports, ship's papers, income tax demands and one toilet roll, "take the bloody lot."

He grinned and picked out those he wanted. Presently he handed the bundle back and gave a curt order to the helmsman.

"O.K. We'll tow you in."

Black faces peered at us as we ran alongside the jetty. Negroes and Indians left their work to come and stare at us. And I believe I heard the boarding officer, Mr Franor by name, mutter to a white man as he stepped ashore, "Frenchmen be damned. They're English."

My first impression of setting foot on shore was that the stelling, as a wooden quay is called in Georgetown, was heaving and pitching under me and that everyone swayed backwards and forwards as I spoke to them.

A negro brought a bucket of lime and ice water, and I fancy I tasted a drop of gin in it. A gulp each and the bucket was empty.

We stood under a fresh-water pump and began to rub some of the salt off our bodies. We were amazed to find that some of the sunburn came off, too, with a little soap and water.

Mulatto newspaper reporters began to arrive. Port officials came to see us in an unofficial sort of a way. Big black policemen kept people away from the boat.

We seemed to have caused a bit of a fuss.

Mr George Benson, the surveyor of customs, arrived and asked us, rather unnecessarily I thought, if we wanted a shave.

We found some musty smelling at trousers and one shirt between the two of us. Lacking a shirt, I had to wear a thick sweater in spite of the fact that it was about ninety in the shade.

Piloted by the good Benson, we strode up through the town, the objects of he much curiosity: Even white folk in cars slowed down to have a second look at tie the strange bearded figures in their midst. They seemed to say "Who the devil are these unshaven ragamuffins?"

The de-bearding was a painful business performed with much patience by a black barber, but once it was over Mr Benson took me along to a drug store to obtain treatment for my injured eye.

We could not wait to buy respectable clothes. Our minds were full of dinners. All the time at sea we had planned a mighty repast—roast beef, Yorkshire pudding (double helpings), apple tart, ice cream, cheddar cheese and—ah—a gallon of beer.

Mr Benson got us on course for the Ice House Hotel. Even minus beards we still looked a bit fierce, but we forgot what we looked like when Mr Benson disappeared and returned with three tots of rum. Three tots, especially two of them, vanished with remarkable alacrity. Then the dinner.

It was not the dinner we had been planning. They didn't know about roast beef and Yorkshire pudding in Georgetown then. And there was no apple tart. But the chicken, yams and rice made a splendid substitute. It all looked pretty good as we'd just come off iron rations.

Mr Benson left us to gorge. In the middle of the table was what we thought to be pickled tomatoes. We plastered the contents over our food and set to.

The pickled tomatoes turned out to be hot peppers — about six times as hot as any pepper one buys in England.

Bully took a mouthful and let out a roar. He stormed round the room, spluttering and coughing, while I clamoured for ice-water.

A waitress came hurrying in, thoroughly alarmed. A jug of ice-water was produced in the nick of time. It looked as though Bully was about to go berserk.

The meal was ruined. Our lips and mouths burned and stung intolerably. We could not bear to eat. There was only one consolation. A gallon of beer, straight off the ice.

We trudged miserably back to where *Thelma* lay alongside the customs jetty. It was dark. As we approached the wharf a voice rang out.

"Halt! Who goes there?"

Little thinking the challenge applied to us and much too shaken up by the effects of the hot peppers, we took no notice. Again the challenge. Still we advanced.

There was the sound of a bolt in a rifle. A figure loomed up out of the gloom and aimed a gun at us. Somewhat bewildered, we made a dash at our would-be assailant, only to find that he was a policeman guarding the rum bond.

Like most Demerara negroes, he was a jovial soul and took it all in good part, but warned us that we had come perilously near to being shot.

After that we always took care to answer his challenge with a call of "friends". Whereupon he would reply "advance friends," and the formality was over.

The Guiana of those days was not a place to look for dreamy romance and lazy days, but for us as strangers it was full of interest. It is a country steeped in a history which should be better known in England — a history of settlers struggling against a malignant climate; of Spaniards wildly marching, fighting and slaughtering in search of El Dorado, the mythical Golden City which was thought to be thereabouts; of attacks and conquests by English sailors; of slave trading and a murderous slave revolt.

Sometimes I stood on the bridge of the ferry steamer *Queriman*, which plied back and forth across the Demerara River from Georgetown to the East Coast. Her master, Captain Phillips, a happy, grey-haired negro of fifty-eight, who had seen many years of seafaring, would point out to me all the interesting people coming aboard his vessel. There would be a party of gold and diamond miners back from the bush, mostly black men and locally known as "pork-knockers". There were young Indians coming to town after travelling for days on foot; planters and overseers from outlying plantations.

Now and then there would be a couple of Englishmen off to the interior to look for gold. Serious-looking fellows clad in old clothes and tattered trilby hats. We met one of these young adventurers, Baldwin by name, who had left England in a ketch named the Southern Pearl, which reached the Galapagos Islands in the Pacific. One by one the crew left her and Baldwin found himself in Guayaquil, in Ecuador, and set about crossing the continent to British Guiana by canoe and shanks' pony. Down the mighty rivers, through the bush and swamps, camping or finding shelter with the Indians, he accomplished a journey which took him across some two thousand miles of South America.

Men who knew the bush said it was a feat to be proud of, but Baldwin's only comment was: "It was easy."

He left in company with a friend named Prodgers to look for gold in the interior.

"And after that?" I enquired as they departed.

Baldwin shrugged his shoulders.

"Maybe I'll get into Venezuela."

I knew that he would not be allowed to walk into Venezuela as he pleased if the authorities knew anything about it, but for a man of Baldwin's resource there is a back door to every country. Venezuela attracted Baldwin. There was gold there, oil and natural plantations. Wild, untouched country.

We met several of these adventurous souls during our wanderings. A common feeling seemed to draw us together. Nearly all were Englishmen.

The Scots were too canny to pursue such a casual life, and colonised in their dour, matter-of-fact fashion. The Scot does not shirk toil and hardship, but he wants something out of it in the end. The Englishman seems quite content to muddle along in any old place, trusting to luck and letting the future look after itself. Only the Irishman seems at all inclined to join him in such sentiments, and one often finds Englishmen and Irishmen abroad partners in some hazardous venture.

Few of these happy-go-lucky souls had any thoughts of home. Years before he sailed in the Southern Pearl, Baldwin had been in the balata business up at Mackenzie City, famous chiefly for its vicious mosquitoes.

Friends we found in dozens at Georgetown. There were sumptuous dinners at Dr Cochran's house. He was the Port Doctor and was the only man in Georgetown at the time who went sailing for pleasure; and that in a little flat-bottomed dinghy with a piece of heavy greenheart wood as a centreboard.

Often we would join a party for a drive around in the country. Once a Portuguese friend, who had been having a few before starting, took us for a hair-raising ride through the outlying villages, and finished up by having a breakdown on a lonely road, miles from anywhere. But for Bully's knowledge of motors and their tricks we might have been there still.

Demerara is below sea level. It was strange to walk along a road and see ships above us putting in and out of port. The Dutch built a great sea wall to shield Georgetown (it was called Stabroek in those days) and but for this the place would have been flooded. Had it not been for the Dutch, whose descendants can still be traced in the capital, it is unlikely that Guiana would ever have been colonised. They seemed to like the place, so reminiscent of their native Holland, except in climate.

How many people know that these Hollanders, driven out by the English, eventually accepted a marshy, mosquito-ridden stretch of land named Surinam in exchange for what is now New York. One cannot help thinking that the Dutch must have been a bit slow when they gathered at the Peace of Breda in 1667.

One day we were told that we would have to visit the Governor at Government House. Here, indeed, was a problem for us. Were we to present ourselves at the holy of holies in canvas slacks and singlets, or were we to lash out on a tailor's order?

A solemn council with friends ashore resulted in our being persuaded to buy a suit of clothes each. The tailor was an Indian with an elastic tape measure.

When the creations arrived Bully's trousers proved to be about three feet too long and stood on his boots like concertinas. The jackets reached almost down to our knees in front and sloped up aft at such a remarkable angle as to be of a type known as bum-freezers.

The tailor was brought on board to review his handiwork. The suits disappeared for three days. Meanwhile the Governor came to see us on his way to the interior, for which he had to leave unexpectedly. So when the tailor returned, full of apologies, with the garments, we told him we didn't want them. At this he nearly burst into tears, and to save a heartrending scene we gave him thirty bob and packed him off, quite happy and content and promising to make any further alterations required.

We wore our suits in public with some embarrassment, until one day a young Canadian observed that they were very much like the uniforms worn by the Salvation Army. That settled it. We returned to our original garb and thereafter refused to wear the Governor's suits except when on watch at night when we were far out at sea. And for that purpose they served admirably.

Once I played cricket at the British Guiana Club, but after meeting C. R. Brown and C. V. Wright, the West Indian test match cricketers, I decided that seafaring was more in my line.

At last it was good-bye to Guiana. Good-bye to all those hospitable folk, to those laughing coloured people and the stern adventurers of the bush.

Lazy days in Port of Spain

Back to sea. Watch and watch; four on and four off, with dog watches of two hours the afternoon and evening. We found that the old seaman's system worked best even with only two of us.

We got away just before sunset and the *Queriman* gave us some rousing shrieks on her whistle as we ran past her for the open sea. It was dark long before we reached the beacon, but the pilots and boatmen were on the look out for us and there was a great ringing of fog bells and hooting of horns as we squared away on our course for Trinidad.

It was a short passage but a treacherous coast, and having crossed the mouth of the great Essequibo we stood well out to sea and picked up a spanking south-easterly breeze. There was a strong current in our favour, too, so that on the second day we made a record run of 145 miles.

Soon the wind left us, and although we sighted Tobago and Trinidad on the morning of the fourth day our prospects of a fast passage rapidly diminished. Slowly we crept along the north shore of Trinidad with the sea so still that we might have been berthed in a quiet harbour.

One night we were sitting peacefully on deck waiting for a breath of wind when we were disturbed by voices, and a rowing boat hove in sight, pulled rapidly by two negroes. They came towards us at great speed and did not rest on their oars until some fifty yards away. They then held a whispered conversation which, in the silence of the calm, we could hear quite plainly. Their hushed voices came across the water as clearly as if they were alongside.

"That ain't her, I tell you."

"Listen, boy. Who else can it be? She'm a sloop and she'm white."

"Well, if you say so, you hail 'em. This fellah ain't."

A quiet call came across the water. We answered and asked their business.

"All ready, sir."

"All ready for what?"

Again a whispered conversation in which one occupant of the boat repeated "I told you so" innumerable times.

Presently we were hailed again.

"Ain't you seen a sloop 'bout here, mister? We'm lookin' for her to give her some water."

We told them we had seen a sloop (as the West Indians call a cutter) becalmed at dusk several miles to the northward; whereupon they thanked us profusely and rowed off hastily in that direction.

They were smugglers.

Next day a light breeze sprang up and the sloop we had seen bore down on us, a white flag fluttering in her rigging as a signal that she wished to speak to us. We backed our headsail and waited.

"Where you from?"

"Demerara."

"Where you bound?"

"Port of Spain."

Six black faces peered at us and presently their spokesman came to the rail again.

"You seen a boat round about here?"

It seemed we had unwittingly taken on the job of smugglers' guide. We told him about the boat we had sent to the northward during the night.

"Well, they sure are silly men. They sure are. Thank you, sir."

And off they went.

It took us six days to make the last fifty miles to Port of Spain, and not without something of a scare after we had negotiated the swirling Boca channel between the islands at the head of the Gulf of Paria. Well on the way into Port of Spain we were becalmed in the fast-running flood stream. Islets and rocks bore down on us and swept by at a disturbing speed. All missed us until we seemed to be drawn into a little archipelago which at the time seemed to spell nothing but disaster.

On the top of one island we saw black convicts breaking and carrying stones under the eye of a taskmaster. At the foot of the rocks they were carrying them waist high into the water, apparently building a causeway. All ceased work to watch *Thelma*'s mad career among the rocks. We had no sweep to pull her out of danger. It had disappeared one night in Georgetown.

Frantically we cut the squaresail from the spars and stood one at the bow and one at the stem to push her off the cliff. Praying that the backwash from the cliff would hold us clear, we kept all sail set lest there should be a breath of wind. If only we had had our sweep we could have pulled the vessel to safety round the point of land on the north side of the island.

Within a few feet of the rocks *Thelma* steadied, and Bully shoved the squaresail boom on to a great boulder and gave such an almighty shove that he nearly landed in the water. With what way he gave her I tried to steer her clear, but she only spun round and headed for the rocks again. I had a fleeting impression of convicts and warders alike gazing down on us from above.

Again Bully plied the spar, but the tide pinned *Thelma* to the foot of the cliff. She had but a couple of yards clearance. Thank heaven it was deep water right up to the shore.

Bully, with his feet against the mast, held his own. The sweat ran off his body and his veins stood out as if they would burst. Then with a terrific heave he pushed her head round and she shot offshore far enough for me to give her helm. She swung again, but this time into the eddy that swirled round the point. We missed some outlying boulders by a matter of inches and—what a relief—we were clear.

As we sighted Port of Spain, a low-lying spot backed by beautiful hills, we crept up to windward of a small sloop.

Anxious to try *Thelma* against the local craft we sailed close up to her, broke out the balloon foresail and made it quite obvious that we felt cocky enough to try to race her into port.

She was a nicely-shaped craft and bore her sail well in a squall, so that for a time there was not much in it. But when it came to working headsails and pegging to windward the West Indian pointed so badly and sagged to leeward so rapidly that we were safely anchored and eating an evening meal before she came past us.

For a man with a head full of ships and sail, Trinidad is a good place. It's a good place, too, for he who likes good rum and genial company.

Anchored in the roadstead we found ourselves neighbours to many a fine schooner. Big three-masters, smartly kept and the pride of their coloured crews. Nearly all the skippers were white, and one of them told me that he always had mulattos from Grenada to work his vessel. One afternoon he sang their praises in a loud and beery voice in a song which I could make neither head nor tail of. I discovered afterwards that the words were in patois.

We met ashore a typical West Indian seaman from the French island of Martinique. He was working as a customs boatman. A tall, powerful fellow, well built, with loose, broad shoulders, he looked very English because of the little short moustache he wore. His face was brown and weatherbeaten but the skin of his body was almost white. His name was Martineau.

He could talk of nothing but ships and the sea. He loved the schooners for they, he said, were his best and truest friends. He could name a schooner as soon as she showed above the horizon; where she was from, what she was carrying and who was her master. Many a time I caught him gazing out across the gulf when I suspected that he should have been busy polishing brass on the customs launch. His body was ashore but his soul was with the ships he saw on the horizon. To Martineau the islands were nothing without their schooners.

He told us of voyages he had made; of the time when he crossed the Atlantic in a schooner to France; of the times he had sailed down Rio way and to Buenos Aires; and how he joined the British Navy in the Great War.

He took a great liking to *Thelma*. He liked the way she went
to windward, the way we came up through the roads in one tack
against an easterly wind.

Great fellow, Martineau, although with his West Indian talk I
could only just understand about half of what he had to say. He
was happy and good-hearted, always helping us to do this or that,
even undertaking the recanvassing of our one and only lifebelt. I
decided that if ever I ran a schooner around the West Indies
(which was not entirely an idle dream) I'd sign on Martineau
first.

On our first visit ashore we were fortunate enough to meet Mr
A. E. V. Barton, Collector of Customs for Trinidad and Tobago,
and a number of customs officials. Soon *Thelma* was berthed
alongside the customs wharf. We said we were staying two days
in Trinidad, just to take on board food water. We stayed seven
weeks! Just as in Demerara, we found the inhabitants hospitable
to an embarrassing degree. They seemed to reflect the climate of
their sunny isle—happy-go-lucky, laughing folk; quick to quarrel
and quick to make friends again. And the stranger is looked upon
as one to be protected and fussed over; to be shown round and
treated with the charming natural courtesy which we English can
never hope to imitate.

The boatmen would sometimes call us ashore to a bottle of
rum at sunset. And what rum! They drank it straight — no water,
except a meagre sip as a chaser. Often it was white, Venezuelan
rum. The first time I knocked one of these back I expected the
top of my head to blow off or else go up in a sheet of blue flame.
Phew! I tried to look calm, but was mighty glad when Martineau
passed the ice-water.

Once we sailed to Caledonia, one of the group known as the
Five Islands in the Gulf of Paria. A jolly crowd of Sea Scouts
accompanied us in their little schooner *Viking*. And there were
several tasty suppers and happy hours at the house of the master,
Mr Conrad Potter.

Had there been a breeze we would have sailed to Patos Island,
not because of any natural attractions about the place, for it lies
like a bare hump of rock at the mouth of the Gulf of Paria, near
the Venezuelan shore. The strange history of the island,
unearthed for me by Mr Potter, lends it a fascination entirely

unexpected in this lonely place.

It seems that the Venezuelans would never admit British sovereignty over the island and included it in their state of Cristobal Colon. And throughout a dispute which dragged on and on for years and years, the sole inhabitant of the island was an old British subject who hoisted the Union Flag every morning on a tall staff. The signalman at Fort George, over Port of Spain, watched for the flag and daily reported to the harbour master that "this morning, sir, Patos Island still belongs to Britain." How many people at home, I wondered, would ever hear of Patos Island and its loyal keeper?

Feeling energetic one morning, and the calm being broken by a few puffs from the east, we got under way for the sleepy little port of San Fernando, in the south of Trinidad. A dreamy town with a sprinkling of Englishmen, Indians and Chinese. My chief impression was of sitting on a shady balcony watching a party of beautiful Venezuelan senoritas being toted round the shops by their numerous chaperons, from whom the wenches seemed frequently to escape. Two of them even escaped as far as our balcony, but we spoke no Spanish and they no English. I tore off to fetch an interpreter but when I returned the birds had flown. Bully just shrugged his shoulders and murmured "me no savvy."

Then to Brighton and Le Brea, where the pitch comes from. Pitch everywhere. Apart from the great pitch lake it seems to ooze out of the very sea shore. We found a tree growing on a half tide reef consisting entirely of black lumps of hard pitch. How the tree kept alive on salt water and pitch is a mystery to me.

Down this way we heard a lot about the hurricane which struck the south of Trinidad before we arrived. It had cleaved a path right through the jungle and tipped a native village all cock-eyed. It was the first hurricane in Trinidad for 400 years. Of course, that would happen because we decided to cross the Atlantic at that particular time. But when I saw the destruction it had caused I was glad that *Thelma* did not catch the full force of it. We must have been far safer at sea than the folks ashore.

There was a little colony of English, Scots and Americans working on the pitch lake, and there was a lot of rum punch absorbed one night in the club house at Brighton. It was the fault of one Jimmy Mathieson that I fell off the pier that night.

Back to Port of Spain at last to get ready for sea again. But the mañana was deep in us and we were days and days considering and talking about the smallest and simplest tasks. We would turn in overnight with great resolves. "Tomorrow we paint the decks, overhaul the rigging, stitch the spinnaker and clean out the forecastle."

We would arise at about seven. An hour would be taken up by a shower bath and a discussion on breakfast. Then Jo, the Indian orange girl, would arrive — three big green'uns for a penny. Sojo would patiently peel the oranges for us until the juice almost ran Out of our ears. Away goes Jo with an empty tray and with only two hours left till noon we would set about making Gulf Stream Hash for dinner. The eating of this invariably produced a state of intense perspiration, and it was necessary for the victim to lie quietly on his back for at least an hour.

A pipe of baccy and a man would come by with ice-cream. This counteracted the hash. An hour of ice-cream and we would struggle up the wharf to swap yarns with our pals over a cup of tea or a bottle of cold beer.

Just before dusk Martineau and his friends would appear with a bottle of rum. Then off to dinner with Mr Barton, Mr Johnson, Mr Potter or the good Mrs Forbes. Mrs Forbes lived in a lovely house at Belmont, and we would disport ourselves on her balcony and watch the tiny humming birds flitting around the bushes.

And at about midnight we would tumble aboard and commence upon a bout of self-rebuke.

"We didn't do that painting."

"No, and we didn't stitch the spinnaker." "Or clean out the forecastle."

"Oh, hell. What's the hurry?"

And that is why we stayed seven weeks in Trinidad instead of two days.

I must tell you about Jimmy Riddle. We had a rat on board. Now one would not think that a rat could hide himself away in a twenty-six-foot boat, but this one did. He emerged at night to eat our flour, our potatoes, our bread and even our sails.

I tried to flood him out by half sinking the boat, but he was hidden away behind the light inside sheathing known as the ceiling.

There was nothing to be done except get a cat. We asked Martineau. Yes, Captain Alec would get us one. Sure enough Captain Alec, a loveable old negro, arrived with a weird looking little mite in his huge black hand. We were assured the object was a he.

The kitten was no bigger than a rat himself, but we established him on board complete with a specially designed sand-box which he stubbornly refused to use. Thus, in view of his habits, we named him Jimmy Riddle. It was not until we were far away from Trinidad that we discovered that James should have been named Jane. But Jimmy it was, so she had to stick by her name.

Before Jimmy settled down to sea life and good manners we had to throw overboard two bolsters (the only ones we had), four blankets, Bully's shore-going jacket and the lino on the cabin floor. After Bully's jacket went he insisted on the cat living almost entirely in the sand-box. But our ship's company was now increased to three.

One night I was ashore with a young schooner skipper. We spent some hours together and demolished considerable quantities of rum. Bully was at the pictures. The skipper became very talkative. So did I. He became very confidential. So did I. We went round such places in the town as would interest two cheerful young men. The skipper seemed to know every inch of Port of Spain. He had been born and bred there.

At last we found ourselves in a musty little Chinese cafe on the east side of the town, a jolly little place with ingenious doors which one could peep over and under without seeing who was inside. It was a place where all sorts of people could be found. Respected white men brought mulatto girls there for a quiet supper. Drunks rolled in for a meal and a sober-up. Venezuelan Spaniards drawled over wine and grapes. Traders talked over business which could not possibly be honest in such an atmosphere.

John Chinaman can be relied upon to keep his mouth shut. No questions penetrate his inscrutability. He would just shrug his shoulders and murmur, "me know nothing."

My seafaring companion seemed to be well known. I noticed

that the attention paid to him was a little more than to the average customer. The drinks were of the best, the supper was superb — curried chicken and almonds. And, as far as I could see, no bills to pay. This seemed very strange.

Presently the skipper beckoned to the proprietor as he padded silently by.

"This is the gentleman I spoke of. He is from England."

The Chinaman bowed with the suspicion of a smile on his face.

"Woo Sang may be able to put business in your way," explained the skipper in a low tone. He had said something about it earlier in the evening.

"What sort of business?" I asked.

"You carry small cargoes from Venezuela," said the Chinaman. "Wines, fruits, fish—all for my restaurant."

It seemed queer that he should offer me cargoes of foodstuffs for no apparent reason, so I played his own game and just nodded. It was for him to do the talking.

Sang had no more to say. He moved off and brought more drinks. As he poured them out with meticulous care he murmured:

"You sit in bad place to talk. You wait here till more people go."

We gulped our beer and waited; waited an hour or more until only a few stray souls occupied the café It was nearly 2 a.m.

Sang came again.

"All people here now I know. All right. We talk."

The skipper, coming rapidly under the influence of alcohol for the second time, cleared the air with a blunt statement.

"Sang wants opium."

"Where from?" I asked.

"Not far," said Sang, quietly. "You take ship across the Serpent Mouth. Fellow see you there. All easy. You bring here. I pay you 300 dollars a pound."

Three hundred dollars for a pound of opium sounded very easy money. True, the stuff was easily detected by its smell, but there was no need for us to bring it right ashore. We could anchor in the roads and Sang could send for it at some convenient time.

Sang went off to serve some new customers. The skipper

nudged me and whispered.

"He'll pay you four hundred if you push him."

Sang returned.

"When you go?"

I pondered. There was Bully to consider. He might not agree. I asked Sang to give me a day to think it over.

"So. I no hurry. You come back here to-morrow. I make nice supper for you. Plenty rum."

We departed without paying any bills and made our way to the wharf. I remember a man in a trilby hat kept appearing at odd moments from street corners. It was always the same man. I saw the skipper taken off to his ship by a boatman and walked back to the customs wharf where the *Thelma* was berthed. For some unknown reason, instead of going straight aboard I retraced my steps and found two policemen talking at the gate with a man in a trilby hat. They bade me a polite goodnight and I repaired on board, a much befuddled and puzzled young man.

Here was I, with one foot in the opium trade and policemen watching me before I had scarcely digested the Chinaman's proposal.

Bloody fool! Twenty years in clink? Not me. Next day I wrote a hasty note to Sang and sent it by a negro boy.

"Leaving for sea tomorrow. Good-bye- and best wishes."

I saw the skipper again before we left. He told me that Sang knew well enough why I turned his offer down. So *Thelma* didn't become an opium smuggler after all.

It took us half a tide to say good-bye to all the folks we knew in Trinidad. By the time all the handshakes were done the ebb was well away and with only feeble puffs of wind in the Gulf we did not clear the Bocas until evening.

The Gulf of Paria is very miserly with its breezes when the trade wind is out of season. The coloured sailormen have a saying: "There's ninety-nine winds in this bay. Make it a hundred and it's a gale." It took me a long time to fathom that statement, but eventually we discovered its meaning by exasperating experience.

The direction of the breeze is likely to change four or five times in an hour, with spells of flat calm interspersed. I have seen a schooner beating to windward up to Port of Spain and another

on her heels with a spanking breeze over the quarter. Hard rain
squalls come from all directions, and once a heavy south-west
wind completely wrecked the customs wharf.

It was good to get back to sea again after our lazy days on the
island. We ran into the trade winds almost as soon as we were
out of the Bocas, a good hard breeze and a long swell coming in
from the east. With a full mainsail and a spinning log *Thelma*
reeled off the miles like a thoroughbred; 480 miles in four days.
Little groups of islands rose up over the horizon and sank down
astern like ghosts. Lights blinked at us and faded away. But for
the occasional lulls in the early morning I feel sure *Thelma*
would have beaten that 145-mile run up the Guiana coast.

On the fourth-day the Dutch island of Buen Ayre loomed up
out of the haze and we altered course for Curaçao. There was a
night of wakefulness dodging the dangerous reef of Little
Curaçao; a lee shore with the current setting strongly towards it,
and I'll swear my heart missed several beats before *Thelma* was
safely round it and heading up for the main island.

With the forenoon sun blazing on the land we sailed gently by
a school of huge blackfish into the stillness of the harbour. The
kindly harbourmaster allotted us a berth near the fort. The
customs made the usual formalities as brief and as palatable as
possible. That is the way with Dutch officials. Days in Holland
taught me that some years before. They can be efficient without
bombast, stern without abuse.

In a waterside tavern we met an Austrian who spoke English
so badly that at times he could not understand himself. He talked
of his adventures after the war, of the times when he had earned a
living as a steeplejack in Holland, as a sailor and a smuggler —
and Lord knows what else.

With some degree of mental strain we followed his chequered
career until he reached Curaçao. At this stage we resorted to
pencil and paper, sundry drawings and a map of the Dutch West
Indies. He told us of a day in June of 1929 when he was startled
by the sound of shooting in the town, of frightened people
dashing into houses and crying, "The Venezuelans have come!"

Apparently an ambitious Venezuelan "general" named Urbina
had revolutionary ideas. He loved revolutions. Not that a
revolution is anything unusual in Venezuela, but Urbino dearly

wanted to have another one. With twenty men he arrived in a cattle schooner and, surprising the sentries outside the fort, held up the soldiers with rifles and revolvers which our Austrian friend swore were loaded only with blank cartridges. (His version is not the only one I heard, for an American sailor told me that he saw the Venezuelans firing off blank shot along the waterfront to scare the populace — which they did very effectively.)

Before the bewildered Hollanders realised what had happened in their sleepy little colony the raiders had seized arms and ammunition from the fort and proceeded to round up all the Venezuelans who lived in the port or were working aboard the many schooners which ran to and from the mainland. "Come with us. We make a big revolution"—and guns were thrust into their hands and they were banded together with Urbino's daring twenty.

But it can never be said that a Dutchman is not brave. The soldiers and police, although covered by the raiders' rifles, launched a sudden and disastrous counter-attack. Dutch blood flowed on the paving stones, Dutch souls went to a Hollander's heaven—but all in vain. The buccaneers had gained the upper hand by their swift blow and all resistance proved futile.

The triumphant Venezuelans marched to the Governor's house and demanded his surrender. The Military Commander was already a prisoner. The distracted Governor was brought forth and the whole company marched down to the docks with their prisoners and boarded an American steamer, the S.S. *Maracaibo*. Urbino ordered the captain to. get under way for the Venezuelan coast, and with a gun in his back he had no option but to do as he was told.

From the parapet of the fort the dismayed Dutch soldiers watched the ship steam out of the narrow harbour entrance. They dared not fire lest the Venezuelans kill their Commander and the Governor. The vessel dipped rapidly over the horizon. The Dutchmen, mulattoes and negroes of the town breathed a sigh of relief.

Curaçao had been conquered and set free in a day. Shades of Harry Morgan!

How the Austrian laughed! He slapped his thigh and nearly spilt his beer when he recounted the embarking of the prisoners in the *Maracaibo*. To him it was all a great joke—and the joke was on the Dutch.

Poor Urbino! After such a daring raid — as daring as any of the buccaneering ventures of days gone by — his revolution fizzled out like a firework in the rain. His attack on the Venezuelan troops was repulsed with great loss. His braves fell like ninepins around him. The recruits from Curaçao fled.

Think of what a name Urbino would have been if he and his associates had culminated their efforts by overthrowing the Venezuelan Republic. What a man to have gone down in South American history!

So to more peaceful subjects — to a day aboard the tanker *Acardo* with Captain Jones of Wales. What a difference to step aboard this great iron ship from our little packet of pitchpine and oak. We stood on the bridge and watched her swing slowly in the oily lagoon; heard the high-pitched cry of her Chinese quartermaster in answer to the pilot's curt orders.

"Starboard the wheel."

"Starboard the wheelo, sir." His cries sounded like a peewit on an English moor.

Instruments galore, telegraphs, mechanical precision — that is modern sailoring. No roaring mates and hours on the yard arm. No hanging on to a dipping bowsprit. No hauling and sweating on sheets and halliards. Just a few clear-cut orders and the ship was under way and out to sea.

"Good night, cap."

"Good night."

And the pilot took us back to the shore in his launch.

The whole business of getting the ship to sea had been accomplished with scarcely a dozen words spoken. Efficiency; organisation. And people say that these steamship men should be trained in sail.

Why? I love sailing ships, but what relation have they to the operation of the modern steamer? It is just as much sense to say that an aviator must first serve in a steamer before he can navigate an aeroplane.

The days of sailoring are over. These men who handle steamships are not seamen in the old sense of the word. They are just ordinary young men trained to do a special job and to do it efficiently. Sailing ships are all right for the hard cases, the die-hards and bloody fools like me. But to teach a man to handle a steamship—put him in a steamship.

But all this is nothing to do with the fact that we cut our stay in Curaçao as short as possible because, owing to our country's lack of consideration for *us*, an English pound only bought twelve shillings worth of beer — and Dutch beer at that, which is mighty like water to an Englishman!

To Panama and the Pacific

Our 700-mile passage to Panama was notable chiefly for our attempts to beat the record day's run of 145 miles. The trade wind was blowing hard and steady and there were times when we deliberately risked our canvas in our efforts to do 150 from noon to noon.

The first day was encouraging, for we did not get under way until evening and covered ninety-one miles by midday. Soon we had rounded the North Monks rocks and were bowling down the Venezuelan coast to the Cape de la Vela.

When we got a close look at the land I took several sights for the purpose of checking our chronometer, which was getting more and more unreliable. In Georgetown we had taken the instrument to the harbourmaster's office so that it could be checked over a period of eight days. But the young harbourmaster was so preoccupied with his own affairs and the staff so scared of him that no one thought even to look at it until the day before I called to take it back. So there was always some doubt about the wretched thing, and I determined to have it put to rights in Panama before starting on any more long passages.

In London it lost only two and a half seconds a day; in Vigo three seconds; in Tenerife one minute sixteen seconds; and now, by the sights of the Venezuelan and Colombian coasts, one minute thirty-seven seconds. We saw the land often enough to check our longitude on this passage, so we were not in any way worried by the temperamental timepiece. The thing was like a woman: dainty and delicate, useful at times, but entirely unreliable.

One morning I was on watch from 4 a.m. until 8 a.m. and as the dawn broke I saw a strange sight in the sky. We were sixty miles offshore and as I looked to the southward there was an outline of land high up above the clouds. For a time I thought that it was a peculiar cloud formation, then, casting this notion aside, put it down to a mirage. This, too, was highly improbable, and I began to think of the effects of the tropical sun on the back of my neck. Perhaps, as Bully suggested, we were really mad and did not know it. After all, we spent most of our time cooped up in a twenty-six-foot boat and if both of us went crackers at the same time neither of us would realise it.

However, I found the solution to this mysterious sight by a close examination of the chart. A wriggly black smudge, like a stray caterpillar, was accompanied by the words "Sierras Nevadas de Santa Marta (17,050 feet)." What I had seen, therefore, was a range of mountains eighty-five miles away. As the sun climbed higher we could make out the snowy peaks, looking like Christmas cakes with icing on. It seemed odd to see snow while we sweated in the burning sun.

Not until midday did the clouds draw a curtain over this wonderful picture, and with their coming the wind strengthened so much that we had to bustle ourselves into activity. The big light weather spinnaker had to come in, but we held on to a full mainsail and as soon as the squalls were past we set the spinnaker again in the hope of making an extra knot or two. The wind came strong and the sea was a little troublesome but we hung on to our spread of canvas, expecting the spinnaker to blow to pieces at any minute.

It was not a gale by any means, but we were carrying a lot of sail for the strength of wind. All night we drove on in a helter-skelter fashion and by eight o'clock in the morning we had covered 125 miles. Another four hours. If we could keep up the six knots we were doing we should beat the record.

Bully took the forenoon watch. He was like a bogeyman. No sooner did he show his nose above the hatchway than the spinnaker carried away in a sudden gust of wind and I had a rare job smothering in the sail before it blew away beyond repair.

Within half an hour we had roughly stitched it up and contrived to set it again, but no sooner had we done this than the wind fell away and all our hopes of a record faded. At noon our position showed that day's run as 131 miles. This was nothing out of the ordinary. We had often done 130 in the Atlantic and there was that 135 down the Portuguese coast. So two very disappointed souls knocked back a dose of Curaçao liqueur, a present from Mr Madura, the British Vice-Consul, and hoped for better luck next day.

But our big spinnaker was ruined until I could get ashore for some proper material to mend it. The tack was blown out completely and the sail needed at least one new cloth. As a useful substitute we used the storm trysail in its place, but 113 and 129 were the best we could do. At last we came in sight of the Colon breakwaters and were promptly becalmed in a damnable swell. The sea was strewn with weed and driftwood, some of which was so dangerous that we had to ward off large logs as they bore down on us on the crests of the waves.

It was not until after dark that the breeze came again and we headed in for the lights of Cristobal docks. More by luck than judgement we found a comfortable anchorage in company with a couple of sturdy old schooners. One of them was a smart-looking vessel named the *Pasajero*, of Roatan (Honduras); little did we foresee the circumstances in which we should meet her again. But that is a tale which must come in its proper place, and for the time being I will tell you of how we hunted iguanas in the bush with a young man named Eddie Borden.

Eddie was a character in Cristobal and Colon. He was a boxer of high repute, in spite of the fact that he trained on beer, a crack rifle shot and an experienced woodsman. Frequently, to the dismay of his handsome Spanish wife, he would go off hunting alone and would stay up in the bush for three or four weeks at a time. How he lived there only Eddie knows, but he had many tales to tell of his hunting expeditions. He knew every insect, snake and animal in the woods.

We were awakened at five o'clock one morning by Eddie's voice on the bank of the old French canal, where some young Americans had found us a quiet berth.

"Say there, you Limies; I'm gonna take you guys huntin'."

So out we tumbled and, armed with a Webley automatic and a home-made shotgun, followed Eddie to the main road where we fell in with one Bill, a six-foot American just back from a long spell in the bush and on his way to the States. Bill was coming with us.

Some miles out of town we turned off by a narrow footpath and tramped towards the bush country ankle deep in mud and water. Soon the path faded into nothingness and often we had to cut our own trail through the vines and branches with machetes. A machete is a survival of the old Spanish sword, slightly curved, and ideal for beating down undergrowth.

To us poor sailors, unaccustomed to much walking, it seemed an endless trudge, and long before we paused for breath my legs were nigh fit to drop off. There was mud and slush everywhere, for the rainy season was but barely over and some of the marshes stank offensively in the heat. Sometimes we could not see the sun for long periods, so thick was the bush overhead, and Bully was just remarking to the world at large on the mentality, character and ancestry of the man who conceived the idea of such an expedition when Eddie called a halt in a grassy clearing on the side of a steep hill.

"There ought to be iguanas in these trees," he said.

Sure enough there were. These iguanas live entirely on leaves and vegetation in the high trees, and because of their colour it is not easy to pick them out on a lofty branch. But Eddie had led us to a good spot. There were hundreds of them.

Bill and I wagered Eddie and Bully as to who would get the most iguanas. Bill had a gun which had cost him 300 dollars and I had a pistol which had cost ten bob. The only iguauna I hit was drilled right through the belly and ran off at great speed along the branches which sloped down into the undergrowth.

In spite of my bad shooting we thought the day was ours. Bill shot down five and I collared them by the tail as they fell. They were big ones, too. But when we met the other two we found them sitting alongside a pile of twelve. So we lost and had to carry them all home.

We were too late in the day to get a wild pig and I was not sorry, because carrying seventeen weighty iguanas through the bush is no joke. But Bill was used to long treks with a heavy pack and he stuffed nine of them into a huge haversack and marched off so fast that we could scarcely keep up with him. Blimey! It was hot work. Ants swarming up my legs, flies buzzing round my ears — I swore I'd finished with hunting from that day on.

Once clear of the bush we made a fire and skinned and gutted the iguanas. A revolting job, even Eddie admitted that, and none of us could picture ourselves eating the ghastly looking carcases which Eddie took home for his wife to cook. But eat them we did, and found to our surprise that properly cooked the flesh looks like chicken and tastes quite good.

It seemed that our destiny was somehow wrapped up in the Isthmus of Panama, for before we were long in Cristobal we ran up against a young man named Hugh Craggs. Craggs knew something of the sea and sail and appeared vastly interested in our doings, particularly as to where we planned to go. Beyond going through the Panama Canal into the Pacific we had no plans at all, for we were both bits of driftwood floating around the waters of the earth in a haphazard and entirely irresponsible fashion. So Craggs started talking of Cocos Island.

When serving in the schooner *Malaya* he had spent forty-seven days there and the place seemed to have fascinated him. Stories of treasure said to have been buried there he had investigated and disproved so far as was humanly possible; yet still this lonely ocean mountain captivated his imagination. He contended that although the island was roughly four miles by six there was less known of the interior than of any island in the Pacific. He had us to his flat one evening and dived into reference files of some seven years' research. We came away dead set on visiting this enchanting and uninhabited isle.

We held conclave, too, with Earle Browne, an American who had been with Craggs in the *Malaya*. Browne was convinced that no one in the world knew as much about Cocos as Craggs. And there were plenty of stories about the place, mostly concerning pirates and buried treasure. There were many versions of how the treasure was supposed to have reached Cocos and many tales- of the futile expeditions made in search of it, and every thread of these yarns had been scrutinised by Craggs with meticulous care.

Every day for months he was in the British Museum without finding a single fact to substantiate these fantastic stories. His enquiries took him to New York and he even got in touch with the Peruvian Government, who were able to inform him that the famous Lima treasure, which was supposedly concealed somewhere about Cocos Island, had never in fact left Peru.

No trace could be found of the characters mentioned in the several stories and no record of the ships concerned. Why, then, do gullible people continue to subscribe to these fruitless expeditions to the island? Think of the money which has been spent on going to Cocos — and who can say truthfully that they have found the slightest indication of treasure?

The plain truth is that the Cocos treasure had become little more than what the Americans call a "racket". So, with no illusions of hidden treasure, we bought a chart of Cocos and determined to call there on our way to the Galapagos islands. The Galapagos are practically waterless in the dry season and Earle Browne told us that the best thing about Cocos was the beautiful, pure water which comes down the mountain side. Well, Cocos would be a good place to fill our tanks before going on to the Galapagos, so one night in Browne's bedroom it was all settled over a crate of beer and a bottle of rum. *Thelma* was Cocos bound.

In the French canal we found a little twenty-two foot vessel, rigged as a schooner and named the *Chance*. She had come from New York and her owner and master was a hardened old Yankee seaman, one Captain Dow. With various companions (a fresh one from every port, it seemed) he had come down through the West Indies, and declared that he was going round the world. Dow was a remarkable character. He was seventy-four years of age and as hard as nails. Strong as a horse and, I have no doubt, a first-class sailorman. He had been in the American Navy when they had sailing ships.

His great fault was that he had several yarns to unload every time he met a stranger, and although they may have gone down all right with a landsman they were nothing but sheer whoppers to us. He had come through three hurricanes, and once the wind blew so hard that it carried away the dinghy from its lashings and drove it from a quarter to half a mile (the distance seemed to vary every time he told his story) before it touched the water. He had beaten a steamship and run 290 miles in a day, carrying 600 square feet of canvas in a gale of wind, this in spite of the fact that we could have stowed any of his sails in our food locker and his jibs were like pocket handkerchiefs. *Thelma* could carry at least twice the spread of sail compared with *Chance* and yet we were unable to set a stitch over 450 square feet. But we just remained dumb and let him ramble on about a fish he had caught which was so big that he had to cut it up into seven pieces before he could get it aboard.

After hearing Craggs on Cocos it was strange to find a ketch anchored over the flats one morning with the red ensign flying, bound for Cocos in search of treasure. She was the *Avance*, a sturdy Bristol Channel type, but none too shipshape in spite of her crew of thirteen.

None were seamen except the skipper, Captain Max Stanton, and his two mates, and with the exception of these three they took little interest in the seafaring side of the expedition. They were after treasure and they were going to get it. There was a spiritualist on board to give them guidance and a metal diviner in case the spirits let them down. The imaginary pirate, Bonito, had already communicated with the medium and told him they would find that which they were seeking. Bonito had also mentioned that the medium would be eaten by sharks four miles from Cocos, but I had confidential information from the forecastle that a waggish member of the crew had had a hand in the conveyance of the message.

They were a tough lot; big strapping fellows. Two of them, whom we were destined to see more of, were named Burwood and Sinsbury. Sinsbury stood six feet six inches and made us look like a couple of midgets. In fact when we went round the town with him we were at the double nearly all the time to keep within talking distance of this long-striding giant. Burwood was a weight lifter and a physical culture expert, and to see him hump things about the ship made work look easy.

On a morning in January the *Avance* took us in tow to go

▲ And thus the great adventure was decided upon.
(Inset: Bob and Bully in even younger days).

▼ *Thelma* on the Thames off Erith.

We found that by eating less we did
not feel so much the craving for water.
Picture taken with an elastic band.

We crossed over to Algeciras to see
the famous bullfighters at Seville.

Jimmy Riddle, third member of the
ship's company after Port of Spain.

Shark – food to augment our stores.

At Balboa. We took care to put a band of copper paint above the Muntz metal sheathing.

 Thelma coming through the Panama Canal alongside Avance.

The last of Thelma, with her starboard side ripped out on the rocks of Cocos island.

Cooknell's shelter on Cocos island,
made from an old sail

Exploring ashore ▶

Sam, in happier mood
▼

▲
The bluenose schooner,
Franklin Barnett

through the Canal. Captain Stanton, who had been mate of the Arctic exploration ship *Discovery II* and looked a seaman all over, was only too pleased to give us a helping hitch through the locks to save us expense. The Canal launches wanted five dollars an hour for towage and it was about a ten-hour job. No thanks. We preferred to wait; and it was a real slice of luck for us to get a free line from. the *Avance*. We only wished that we could disillusion them as to the prospects of their expedition. Stanton had little to say about it. He was just the skipper and I think he had ideas of his own on the treasure business anyway. His agreement was that when the expedition was over he would get the ship. The ethers didn't mind that because they would, by that time, all be millionaires!

To Bully and me it seemed that Stanton had played his cards wisely and made the best bet.

A passage through the Panama Canal was full of interest and wonderment for us, yet I find it a difficult business to write about. The great feats of engineering which the Americans had achieved across this narrow strip of land are on too large and too grand a scale for me to describe.

The huge Gatun locks lifted us eighty-five feet above sea level and deposited us in the artificial lake which covers what was once nothing more than woods and bush. In the first lock we had some flurried moments when the operators started letting the water in, for it bubbled beneath us with such force that we were slewed away from the *Avance*'s side and hove over at such an angle that our rail stanchions were broken and cleats carried away like matchwood. The *Avance*, too, swung wildly about and banged her quarter against the concrete wall. Luckily our damage was only superficial but the pilot aboard the *Avance* addressed a string of blistering Yankee epithets to the men ashore, and thereafter the water was let in at a speed more conducive to the safety of a small vessel.

We set a bit of a sail in Gatun Lake to ease the towline, and our passenger, a young Californian on his way from Cristobal to keep a tryst with a lady in Balboa, devoted himself to some patient but fruitless fishing.

There were Pedro Miguel and Miraflores locks to negotiate before we were down to Pacific level, and it was dusk before the

Avance let us go, shouting a cheery "see you at Cocos" farewell.
It had taken us ten hours to cover forty-eight miles from the
Atlantic to the Pacific.

We drifted on the ebb tide to an anchorage off the Balboa
Boat House and next day set about the business of refitting for
our voyage into the Pacific. There was no need to hurry as the
dry season wind from the North had not yet set in. *Thelma* was
beached for scrubbing and painting and we took care to put a
band of copper paint above the Muntz Metal sheathing to prevent
the teredo worms from getting into her topsides when she was
loaded deep with stores and water.

The work of refitting took us nearly a month to complete. Our
fresh water capacity - the limits of which had taught us a lesson
in our Atlantic crossing - was increased to ninety gallons and we
took on board three months' stores. Tinned food, which was so
cheap in the Canal Zone, was piled up on the bunks for lack of
somewhere else to store it, and for sleeping space we just left
room for one man to stretch himself out on the floor. A wine
barrel was sawn in half—one half being filled with potatoes and
the other with onions. A businesslike portion of salt beef hung in
the galley and 100lb of ship's biscuits were put into drums and
sealed up with solder. Flour, split peas and sugar were stored in
airtight candy tins.

Almost every day Americans would come on board to look at
our vessel and many of them expressed harsh criticism of her rig
and shape. Even allowing for the tastes of the Americans and
their liking for spoon bows and pretty counters, we could not let
them sit there and run down a proven vessel. The long bowsprit,
pronounced a positive danger at sea, was really an asset; for
when going to windward in heavy weather it allowed the jib to be
set at so sharp an angle that the wind got underneath it and
helped the vessel to lift her head over the dangerous breaking
seas. The flat transom stern, which one of these armchair
admirals said was not suitable for running before a following sea,
had served us well on the way to Georgetown when we had to
run out of the hurricane which hit Trinidad. This, combined with
her straight stem and long keel, made the boat so short-ended that
it was almost impossible for her to whip or strain in bad weather.

It seemed so foolish for them to sit aboard there in the flat calm which hung over Panama Bay and pull to pieces design which had been developed through the years of hard experience off the storm-bound Cornish coast. The only American who appreciated *Thelma*'s lines was a man who never saw her. He had served an apprenticeship in a hard-mouthed sailing ship and knew no home but the sea. I showed him a photograph of *Thelma* when I met him some months afterwards aboard the schooner *Cimba*. He squinted at the picture for a moment and then announced in his hearty, booming voice, "Say, that's a fine little vessel. I like the look of her." And from a seaman, that's enough.

Between times of fitting out at Balboa we were able to explore the surrounding country with a friend named Vincent Wirt. We went to Old Panama, the scene of the courageous deeds of the Welshman, Harry Morgan. Only a few grass-grown remains stand to hold the story of the buccaneer's famous raid; only a few tumbling stones to mark how a thousand Englishmen captured a great city after a perilous journey across the fever-stricken isthmus. Rogues and outlaws, no doubt, but heroes just the same. Valiant deeds and untold bravery brought them ample excuse for the cruelty and debauchery which followed their success. Such excesses were but the order of the day among all fighting races.

Wirt took us to see Madden Dam, a gigantic construction being built across the Chargres River, and many were the evenings we yarned over boats, designs, sails and seafaring in his quarters at Ancon.

In the course of our refit we held council on the prospects of acquiring a small dinghy to get ashore at such islands as we might visit. Up to now we had managed without this extra encumbrance, but with the prospects of anchoring in little-frequented places it was essential that we should come by one somehow. We could spare little money to buy a proper skiff, and for a time we wandered round the beaches of Panama in search of an Indian cayuca.

A cayuca is a dugout canoe, and they vary in length from seven feet to twenty. We even saw one lying off Panama City rigged as a three-masted schooner, though how her crew ever made her sail I could not imagine.

But one day we boarded the motor yacht *Alpha*. Tied up at her

stern was the very dinghy that we required. With a little
reduction of freeboard it was small enough to find a place on
Thelma's deck. To cut a long story short the *Alpha* was due to be
hauled up for re-planking. The worm had run riot in her bottom.
The owner offered us the job of getting her high and dry on a
place called La Boca beach. One of those dirty, mosquito-ridden
beaches, full of fleas and sand flies.

Four days we laboured, heaving great baulks of timber into
place to form slipways; and at last, with the aid of miles of rope
and tackle, the great black hull stood high and dry two feet off
the ground. Our reward was ten dollars and the coveted dinghy.

Before we put to sea we made the acquaintance of a grand old
character named Fred Whaler. Every one knew Whaler as the
finest fisherman in Panama Bay. He knew every rock and creek
from the Galapagos to Costa Rica, and many a sound word of
advice did he pour into our ears over a glass of beer down in
Panama. Baits to use, fish to watch for, and, most important of
all, how to catch them. In a cosy little beer garden I learned more
about dolphin, sail-fish, tuna, jack, sharks, whales and black-fish
than I ever thought I could store in my muddled head. The night
before we sailed, Whaler appeared on the causeway loaded with
spoon-bait, lines, ammunition, tropical medicines and more
advice. It was a tough business saying good-bye to old Whaler.

Our fitful chronometer had at last been brought to a
dependable state by the kindness of a man whose name we never
knew. We took the chronometer to the Canal Instrument Repair
Shop and I nearly threw a fit when they looked it over and said;
"Twenty Dollars."

It was too much. We could ill afford it and decided that we
would have to use dead reckoning longitude and make all our
landfalls by latitude sailing. Twenty dollars! My God! But the
Canal people are like that. The impression which most strangers
receive from officials is that they are harsh, money-grabbing
people without a spot of humanity anywhere in their Yankee
hearts. But impressions are misleading.

True, the Canal Zone, officially, was an inhospitable place.
When the officials made things hard all sorts of people would go
out of their way to help you to circumvent the barriers of red
tape. So it was that when the chronometer man in the Repair

Shop heard that we could not afford the twenty dollars to have our instrument repaired, he took us Out of hearing of the man at the desk and said he would take it home with him and fix it up.

A week later we received the chronometer in perfect order, regulated to half a second a day. On such rating, said our friend, the instrument was worth 450 dollars. So it was with the greatest care and tenderness that I shepherded it back to the Boat House. We also had a watch rated to four seconds a day and we were able to keep a log of comparisons between the two timepieces.

For those who might contemplate a voyage in a small vessel the advice of our friend in the Instrument Shop is that three good watches are much more serviceable than one expensive chronometer. If all are properly rated two of them will always check on the third.

The morning of our departure the Hydrographic Office gave us packets of forms for current reports, weather observations, bottle papers and heaven knows what in the hope that we would fill them up for the benefit of mankind during our voyage.

Meeting with The Thing

We sailed on a Friday.

Down through the enchanting isles of Panama Bay we wound our way with a brisk north wind on our quarter. Balboa and its fort at Amador disappeared from view. In its place came little blobs of green and grey which bear such charming names as Taboga, Taboguilla, Bona, Otoque—one-time refuges of Spaniards in flight from the English buccaneers. It is said that many a Jesuit treasure has been hidden on these islands, and those who hunt for gold would do better to explore such places than go on a wild goose chase to Cocos.

The Gulf of Panama is an infamous place for sailing ships because of its deadly calms and swiftly running tides and currents. No place for any seaman who wants a breeze of wind. But our long stay in Balboa had been to good purpose. The north wind had set in and by night-time blew so hard and fresh that the spray flew over us and we were glad of sweaters and oilskins. Four — five — six knots; and there we held it with a single reef in the main and a short breaking sea astern that sent my mind flying back to the days in the North Sea.

We were running at about six and a half knots and heading for Cape Mala light. I turned in for the middle watch and asked Bully to call me as soon as the light appeared so that I could lay a new course to avoid Iguana Island, a low-lying patch of land without light or buoy to indicate its whereabouts at night. I had a call sooner than I expected. Bully, who was dog tired and sleepy through the concentration required in running under mainsail before a strong wind, had not noticed the Mala light flashing on the lee side. He called me out to see a black mass for which we were running helter-skelter in a turmoil of sea. It was Iguana Island.

Down helm and round we came to put *Thelma*'s head to weather. To claw off the land we had almost a gale of wind and a sluicing tide to beat against. With only a single reef in the main, which was safe enough running before the wind, we were over-canvassed when the vessel was brought close-hauled. Pitching and bucking, *Thelma* heeled over until her lee deck was a cascade of surging water. It would be of no use, and indeed there was no time, to reduce sail. We needed every stitch she would bear to make headway. Each time a sea hit her we could feel her halt in her mad career and then go tumbling on again like a frightened mare.

In such circumstances as these the seaman's heart is with his ship. She seems to be striving and straining like a living thing to try to get out of danger. She wants human help at the helm to ease her over the worst of the seas and to drive her hard in the smoother patches. Man and ship work in unison to escape destruction.

For an hour it was doubtful whether we were making any appreciable progress, but at last the bearing of that ominous lump against the horizon began to alter. We were getting clear. I felt a great load taken off me, for if we had had to make a tack towards the mainland we should have lost what little we had gained and might not have weathered the island. We could lay clear on the port tack, and I wished that those critics from Balboa could have seen how *Thelma* brought us out of the situation. She made five miles in an hour against such a wind and sea as would cause a less sturdy vessel of her tonnage to founder without a fight. Not a thing carried away, even though we set a full foresail to keep her going.

We rounded Cape Mala at dawn. A good name for a place with such an evil reputation. It's hell in bad weather and worse in calm. So hard did it blow that we had to stow our mainsail and revert to our old combination of trysail, fore and jib. Thus it was that our first day's run, through a region noted for its calms and vexatious weather, was 124 miles.

Soon we came under the lee of towering Morro Puercos, and that was the last we felt of a respectable breeze for many a day to come. By morning it was deathly calm and we rolled and wallowed in the swell while a constant stream of steamships passed majestically by, bound to and from the Canal. It was noon the next day before we could set our mainsail to a fitful breeze, and although our course led us away from the land the mountainous coastline was still plainly visible in the evening. Towering above all was the great peak of Mariato, 5,000 feet high.

Another day of gentle puffs and Mariato still looked like a sentinel on our northern horizon. It seemed as though we could not get away from it. Once we dropped it below the skyline, only to drift round in a circle and catch sight of it again four days later. No longer did I enter "day's run" in the log at noon. It became "day's drift".

The sea was so calm that not even a gentle swell disturbed its placidity. One evening, just before our last sight of the steamer traffic, we watched the wash of a ship come towards us from some three miles off. It was quite different from the Atlantic calms where the steady roll keeps one in constant anticipation of a breeze. The Pacific doldrums are almost uncanny. It is as if you have been transported into another world, so still and flat is the ocean.

Deep down below us we could see strange fish swimming lazily in the shade of our vessel. Fish such as we had never seen before but which we could identify from Whaler's tuition. We got out our harpoon and hooks. Here was food to augment our stores.

A yellow-tail came up under our stern. I balanced myself on the taffrail and let go at him with the harpoon. It was a straight shot but the barb did not get home and he dived away with a portion of flesh missing from the middle of his back. I tell you this because this injured fish followed us for twenty-four days, and we were able to watch his wound heal up until no trace of it could be seen. But never again did he come within range of the harpoon or venture near a baited hook.

One night we caught a big dolphin on a trailing spoon-bait

and there was enough flesh on him to feed us for a couple of days. But two days of dolphin is a bit monotonous, so much of his carcass was hove back again. This brought the sharks round; great ugly brutes from seven to about fourteen feet long; and the poor old dolphin disappeared in less time than it takes to tell as these hungry beasts tore at the sinking body. And with the sharks came the Old Wife, as the negroes call it; a vicious-looking little fish which propels itself by moving a dorsal fin and a belly fin instead of the usual side fins. The Old Wives were an easy mark for the harpoon as they would come right alongside as if to squint at us and presented themselves as a point blank target. Nice and tasty, too, straight from the water into the frying pan.

Often we would be disturbed by a resounding bump on the side or the bottom of the boat. At first we were seriously alarmed, and rushed out on deck to see what had happened. Nothing to be seen. We hazarded that perhaps we had grazed a piece of driftwood. There being no wind we retired once more to our books and magazines. Once again— another terrific bump.

We threw down our books and jumped for the cabin door. But we both jumped at the same time and jammed each other in so that before we had disentangled ourselves and reached the deck there was no sign of what caused the collision. Mystified, neither of us could suggest the wildest explanation. No piece of driftwood would vanish so quickly, and to be hit twice in a matter of a few minutes would mean that there was plenty of flotsam in the vicinity. Yet not a stick or branch could be seen, and we peered over the side for signs of sunken wreckage. An hour later there was another bump and we were on deck that time; yet not a thing could be seen and we just shook our heads and said "Well I'm — — — !"

It was not until two days later that we discovered the cause of these mysterious concussions. We were manning the rail with harpoon and tackle in the hope of getting a huge shark which was cruising back and forth astern of us. We were watching for a chance to throw when he suddenly dived and came upwards towards us at top speed. Twisting his body over, he hit our starboard bilge with a hefty wallop and dived again out of sight.

From time to time other sharks came up and did the same thing, and we found that they were attempting to knock off the

parasitic sucker fish which clung to them by a sort of rough plate
on the head. Some of these sucker fish grow as much as nine
inches in length, but, being too lazy to swim themselves, they
take free rides on sharks, porpoises, rays, or any big fish they can
find. I remember Whaler telling me that the reason why big fish
and porpoises often leap high Out of the water is that they are
attempting to shake off the various parasites which irritate them.

The shark mystery was not the only one to puzzle our heads.
As I turned out to relieve Bully one morning he reported that
before daylight he had heard strange noises coming from out on
the port quarter. "Like the lowing of a cow," he said, "or an
elephant with asthma."

Being unable to suggest an answer to this second riddle, I
dismissed the matter from my mind, and thought no more of it
until several nights later.

We were lying becalmed. I was keeping the graveyard watch
— the watch in which old seamen say that queer things are likely
to happen. Queer things did happen, too, for as I sat half dozing
in a corner of the cockpit I heard a splash not far away from the
boat. It was a starry night but no moon, and I peered into the
darkness in a sleepy sort of a way. There were many things that
might cause a splash, a jumping fish, a dolphin or a shark lashing
its tail — bust, seeing nothing, I returned to my dozing.

Hardly had my thoughts begun to wander again when
something happened which made me nearly jump out of my skin.
Right behind my back there was a terrifying roar.

Whales, sea serpents, nightmares, all flashed through my
mind in a second as I leapt to the side of the boat to see what
awful creature was upon us. There was a gurgle of water — and
once more the great silence of the calm. I could only make out a
ripple not far from us, as if some large object had sunk to the
bottom. Not another sound did I hear.

Bewildered and, I must confess, a little nerve-shaken, I sat
down again so consumed with wild thoughts that I allowed my
pipe to go out and kept watch long past the appointed time.
When at last I remembered to call Bully I told him of my
experience, fearing he would laugh and say that I had been
dreaming. On the contrary he listened to my story sympathetically
and recalled the noises he had heard some three nights before.

We guessed at big fish, whales and mammoths of the sea without any sort of conviction, and eventually gave the problem up as beyond our comprehension. Our roaring guest we called The Thing, for lack of any other name, and set about catching stray puffs of wind once more with all the variations of sail we could think of.

If anything of a roll disturbed us we found a very effective combination for fair winds by stowing the mainsail and setting two spinnakers. This was by no means a new idea, as it had been the subject of much bar-thumping in arguments on deep-sea rigs for small vessels. Our brief experience was that while it was useful and efficient when there was not enough wind to keep the mainsail and squaresail from slatting, the spinnakers did not give enough sail aloft. Huge, specially made spinnakers would have to be carried to put the scheme into operation properly, but when it comes to having specially designed sails for every sort of weather there is no end to the business. It savours of the summer regatta.

Again our breeze-catching was interrupted by a visit from The Thing. This time it was just past sundown and I was cooking supper in the galley when Bully stuck his head in the hatchway and said: "Come out here and listen."

With the frying pan in one hand I clambered out on deck and we stood quietly in the deathly stillness. Presently from far away on the eastern horizon came a muffled moan. It was as if some huge creature was drawing breath and letting it out with a mighty roar.

"Hear that?"

Another silence.

"There it is again."

It was louder, too. Coming our way.

The frying pan grew cold. The chips set hard in the fat—and still we stood motionless, listening. For several minutes nothing happened, and I could not prevent the comic side of the situation from crossing my mind. There were we two lonely souls who only a few months before had jostled shoulder to shoulder with London's daily multitudes, standing on the deck of a twenty-six-foot boat in the far Pacific, listening, watching and waiting for that which we knew by no other name than The Thing. Who would have thought that such a change could have come upon us, from catching trains and jumping buses to these eerie goings-on in a quiet ocean? It was all too much like a bad dream.

While my mind was thus diverted Bully grabbed me by the arm.

"Look, quick."

Again the hollow breathing followed by a bellowing which seemed less than fifty yards away. In the gathering gloom I caught a glimpse of something white rising above the surface and before I could make out what it was it was gone again. Away to the southward we heard another bellow, faintly this time, for it must have been a long way off.

I returned to the galley to rejuvenate the chips. Bully lit the binnacle light; but neither of us could keep our thoughts from the bellowing apparition we had just seen. The next day, it still being calm, I proceeded to occupy myself with a jig-saw puzzle, much to the delight of Jimmy who danced round with the pieces like an animal possessed. No sooner would I construct the figure of a voluptuous Eastern maiden than James would leap upon it, scatter it all afar and dash out of reach with the feline imitation of a Cockney raspberry.

So I gathered up such bits as she left me and went out on deck to catch some tiddlers to keep her quiet. These tiddlers (forgive the expression, Whaler) tumbled and frolicked around us so thickly that we could scoop them up with a saucepan. I took hold of the necessary utensil, and, followed by the expectant Jimmy, went aft to hang over the stern. But Jimmy got no fish that day. Something happened to make me forget my fishing.

I was holding myself ready to make a scoop when I heard a noise so close that I nearly fell into the water with fright. It was the roar of The Thing.

There, close to us, a shiny white body broke the surface; a great white snout appeared above the water. It was a porpoise.

Not an ordinary porpoise such as grunts. and gambols in the English Channel; not even the usual black or grey in colour. This was a huge thing of mottled white. So big that I only recognised it as a porpoise by its snout. Every time the animal came to the surface to breathe the very sound of it was as loud as the lowing of a cow.

And, as everybody knows, porpoises go about in schools. Not so this one. He went alone. He must have been a mile away before we saw him break surface again and emit an awe-inspiring roar.

So ended the mystery of The Thing.

These excitements helped to make interesting what would otherwise have been a dreary and tedious passage. The weather was so calm and the winds so fickle that we crept south as far as four degrees thirty-five minutes of latitude, only 275 miles above the equator, in the hope of finding a regular breeze. It was an improvement, however small, for we found a light easterly wind which came languidly over the water every night during the middle watch. Sometimes we felt it in the afternoon as well, so that one day we actually made fifty-five miles. But generally we were satisfied to run twenty, and many a day the amount of our progress was almost imperceptible. So we just went on with our fishing, reading and dreaming and began to wonder if a real wind had ever blown in these parts at all.

On our twenty-first day at sea, it had been so calm and still that it was not necessary to keep watch, even at night. So we both slept a full eight hours stretched out on the foredeck. It was too hot to sleep below. Bully had various interruptions, for apart from Jimmy's persistence in seizing his toes as they emerged from the bottom of the blanket, a wee gull perched on his hip and with his head cocked aside regarded the slumbering mate with an air of curiosity.

I told Bully to lie still and open his eyes. At that moment the gull forgot his good manners and roused Bully to irate words and murderous intent. But the gull merely fluttered aft and perched on the taffrail, where we found him in the morning; Jimmy may have had some evil intentions of his own as he crept towards our little visitor but as soon as the bird moved the cat showed a lamentable lack of courage by beating a hasty retreat. This gull bore us company for several days.

Before the sun rose too high to scorch us into inactivity we would take turns with the harpoon and the gun. Fish were always following us, some of them for days on end, and many were marked with the mis-hits of the harpoon or speckled with the discharge from the shotgun. There was our little yellow-tail

recuperating astern; a dolphin with a hole in his back; a shark
with half a dorsal fin shot off; and a long ugly fish something
like a barracuda (I think it is called a wahoo) which was well
ballasted with a .32.

Little black-and-yellow sea snakes would come wriggling
round on the surface, and I am told that they are deadly
poisonous. Bully showed that he was something of a crack shot
with a pistol by knocking the head off one at about twenty-five
yards' range. But when the snake was dead no shark and no other
fish attempted to eat it, as is their custom with any other dead
thing.

The rising of the sun brought a burning heat in the forenoon,
and although there was not a breath of wind we kept our mainsail
set to give us a little shade on deck. A breakfast of fish and chips
and then a few odd jobs necessary to keep the vessel in proper
trim. Bully made a minor alteration to the backstays; I repaired
the big jib which blew out off Georgetown. Then we both set
ourselves to washing down the decks and cleaning out the cabin.

Dinner time. Gulf Stream hash and an hour's sweat to follow.
An afternoon of reading. Yarns and perhaps a croaky song or two
in the dog watches. A glorious sunset; supper — and another day
was done.

On the twenty-second day we were still seventy miles from
Cocos and had begun to head northwards to look for our
destination. Cocos is probably one of the loneliest spots in the
world, for although it lies only a few hundred miles from Central
America it is away from the track of shipping, either steam or
sail, uninhabited and in the doldrums all the year round. It is
possible for a vessel to pass within three miles of Cocos in a rain
squall and never see the island in spite of its two peaks of 2,800
and 1,500 feet. A rain squall or a haze over the island wipes it
clean off the map.

So it was that we were rather fortunate in seeing it as we did.
We had to shape a course for it on a longitude run instead of the
simpler method of sailing along the latitude; and for the accuracy
of this course we had to thank the man who repaired and rated
our chronometer in Balboa. The result was fascinating.

On the appointed day at the appointed time a hazy patch
appeared on the north-western horizon, and before the day was

ended both peaks of the island were plainly visible. This was on the twenty-fifth day. We had hopes of setting foot on shore the next morning, but a strong current setting to the north-east and a spell of windless weather hung our passage out another two days. And just before we reached the island I was foolish enough to lose the harpoon, the most valued of our fishing gear. A shark had been bumping us persistently and I was determined to show him where he got off. I was waiting for him when he came up right beneath the poised harpoon. With all my might I plunged it into his belly as he turned over to bump our side and out went the line as he dived, leaving a patch of blood on the surface. Down, down he went until there was only a fathom of line left on board. I took a hasty turn and waited for the jerk. The line held.

Up he came, faster than I could haul in, and just as I was counting on a set of false teeth for my old age he executed a remarkable manoeuvre by leaping almost out of the water and catching the line in his mouth. That was the end of my part in the battle. He bit the line clean through and sheared off.

As the sun went down on our last night at sea we hove-to a few miles from the shore, because we wanted to make the anchorage at Chatham Bay in daylight. High up on the land a light flickered. We guessed it to be the *Avance* party, resting from their treasure-hunting labours. At least we should meet old friends on this otherwise deserted isle.

Strange Forebodings

As the brilliant tropical dawn broke over the island we put *Thelma* before a gentle breeze and headed in for Chatham Bay. Away to port little offshore rocks dotted the steep-to coast and to starboard there loomed the great hump of Nuez Island, which is separated from the main island by a narrow deep-water channel. Nuez is nothing but a barren piece of rock covered with bird droppings and presenting a most deserted and forlorn appearance.

As we crept forward strange fish came round to take the place of those which had been following us — fish which, even with the help of Whaler's teaching, we could not identify. Some were small and brilliantly coloured with blue and yellow stripes; others were of dark blue or black and darted about so quickly that it was scarcely possible to determine their real size or shape; baby sharks came up saucily on our quarter, soon to be followed by their old man, a huge brute of some fifteen feet in length, the biggest we had seen.

Overhead gulls and booby birds screamed protests at our arrival and aimed their droppings at our unprotected heads. There

was a strong current running to the north-east, and the breeze was
so light that we had to carry a spinnaker all the way into the bay.
Soon we had made out the masts of a vessel lying at anchor and
immediately dubbed her as the *Avance*, particularly as we caught
a glimpse of her black hull wallowing in the rollers. But as it
grew lighter it appeared that she was schooner rigged and in no
way resembled the sturdy old vessel which had towed us through
the Panama Canal. There was no sign of the *Avance* anywhere.

What business, then, had this strange black schooner lying off
an uninhabited island so far from the track of the trading vessels?
It was a long time before we were to know, so many different
tales did we hear of her.

We handed our spinnaker and Bully got the ground tackle
ready as I sounded into five fathoms, a short distance shorewards
of the schooner.

"Down jib."

An unoiled block squeaked at the masthead as the sail came
smartly in. Bully had handled that jib so often while
manoeuvring in narrow waters that he had brought the business
to a fine art. No fisherman could make a smarter job of handling
that sail, and hardly had I given the order than Bully sang out.
"All ready."

I hauled in the mainsheet and put my helm hard a'starboard.
Thelma shot up over a patch of sand which I had caught sight of
a few moments before, and lost way right over the top of it.

"Let go."

Splash! She lay still for a moment and then began to drift
astern as Bully paid out twenty fathoms of chain. Heavy three-
eighths-of-an-inch chain, from a big Whitstable smack. We
stowed the headsails and put the porridge on the stove. Jimmy
woke up and paraded around the deck with an air of approval.
The birds ceased screaming. All was quiet. Yet as I pottered
round the deck I had a feeling of uneasiness. The bay was bound
by rocks which ran out under the water from the foot of the cliffs.
Long rollers were coming in and breaking savagely on shore.
Great lumps of coral made strange patterns on the sea bed. I lay
on my belly and looked over the bow. Down through the clear
water I could see our anchor firmly embedded in the sand, an
object of curiosity for the swarms of fish.

It was an open anchorage and no place for rough weather, but being so calm it did not seem that there could be the slightest danger in lying there for a few days. It would not take us long to top up our water tanks and get away for the Galapagos. It was only those queer fancies of mine that made me dislike the place, and I even went so far as to reveal my thoughts to Bully as he stirred the porridge in the galley with a sweaty hand.

"I don't like this place much."

"Want to move further out?"

"No, she's as safe here as anywhere with the hook in this patch of sand."

"Well, what don't you like about the place?"

"Dunno. Just a hunch."

And with that I tried to cast my fears aside and set about tidying up the ship. But all the same I did not stow the mainsail and left it with just a single gasket round it in case it should be needed in a hurry.

Moreover, I took three very careful bearings of the shore and entered them in the log book. I showed these to Bully and he promised that if at any time he noticed the smallest alteration he would let me know immediately. Having done so much I felt a little more at rest and decided to lay out a kedge anchor later in the day, when we should know more about the conditions of the anchorage.

The island looked very beautiful from where we lay. Wild jungle, coconut groves and a pretty little rock-strewn cove to the westward; a grass-topped hill, some 400 feet high, close to the shore; and inland the towering mountainside, mysterious and unexplored. Craggs had not overstated the island's attractions. The dullest of minds would stir to its strange fascination.

As we came on deck to cool off from the porridge we saw a lot of dirt come slithering down the hill by the shore. We watched for several minutes and presently a negro appeared on the summit wheeling a barrow-load of soil down the slope. Presently another figure appeared. We waved and shouted but they took no notice of us. The first man brought another barrow-load, and having discharged it as before the two men disappeared. They did not show themselves again.

Our dinghy was lowered into the water and immediately

commenced to fill itself with Pacific Ocean. It had been bottom-up in the sun so long that all the joints and seams showed daylight and the water squirted through in a series of fountains. We tied the painter to the taffrail and let her descend to sea level in the hope that after being submerged for a short time some of the leaks would take up with the swelling of the wood.

In the meantime I altered my ideas about a kedge anchor. We were not so lavishly equipped as to have two anchor chains and our custom was to lay out a kedge on a stout manilla warp. As our two-inch tripping line had already chafed through on the jagged bottom in the matter of two hours I felt it would be useless to use a kedge on a warp.

After solemn deliberations we decided that if the anchor chain did not hold her it was quite certain a chafing warp would not. Likewise it was impossible for our main anchor to drag. It could not drag from that patch of sand because it was surrounded by mushroom coral. This mushroom coral grows some little way off the bottom and spreads out according to its name. Thus if the anchor dragged. the lower flukes would go under the coral and hold there so fast that it would be unlikely that we should ever get it up again.

So there did not seem to be much danger of *Thelma* dragging her anchor especially as the weather was dead calm and there was no current to speak of in the bay itself.

To replace the chafed-through tripping line we buoyed the anchor with some pieces of wood so that the straight up and down buoy line would not come into contact with the coral. This we found satisfactory, and we felt that *Thelma* was as safely anchored as she could be in the circumstances. If we had been possessed of plenty of chain I would not have hesitated to have laid out all three anchors. But rope was no good, so we trusted to the heavy chain and bower.

At last, after much bailing, the dinghy was pronounced fit to go ashore in. It would just hold the pair of us, and allowed about six inches of freeboard with Bully's thirteen stone in the stern. I took the oars, one of which was twice as long as the other, and proceeded shorewards. A gentle swell lifted us as I paddled along in a leisurely way, and we thought that all we should have to do would be to step out of the boat as she grounded.

Poor misguided souls.

Bully suddenly craned his neck to twice its normal length and cried:

"There's a man running along the beach!"

I stopped rowing and looked round. There was a half naked figure waving frantically to us to row in his direction. We changed course accordingly and as we neared the shore we saw that the point for which we had been making was a seething mass of surf which broke over sunken rocks and spelt destruction for any boat which might try to land there. And just outside the line of breakers great sharks cruised back and forth, lashing their tails and no doubt smacking their lips before we headed away in response to the signals from the shore.

We assumed that the figure on the beach was one of the men we had seen on the top of the hill and that he had come down to direct us to a landing place. He waded out and soon we saw that he was being smothered by surf which was breaking just as savagely on this strip of sand as on the rocks elsewhere.

He beckoned to us to row straight for him. We reached the line of breakers. No one would suspect from seaward that the surf was piling so high. We were picked up and poised in the air like a cork. The boat spun round. It was impossible to control her. Over she went and out we shot in a welter of white foam.

Thud! I landed on my backside on the hard sand. Just as I drew breath another wave broke over me and half filled my lungs with salt water. In the midst of my spluttering I heard a shout.

"Look out!"

Above the thunder of the breakers I heard Bully echo the warning. On the next breaker came the dinghy, bottom up. I looked up and saw it high above my head. I scrambled away as it crashed down a few yards away. Bully's dripping head appeared above the water. Someone was shaking me by the hand.

"My name's Gooknell. Pleased to meet you. Looked as though that skiff was going to brain you."

I gazed into a sunburnt face, shrouded by long hair and a ginger goatee beard. He presented a wild figure but spoke with a reserved, cultured accent.

"Pleased to meet you," I said, "my name s . . ." Swish! We were both carried off up the beach on another breaker. So the formal introductions were postponed and when we recovered we set about grabbing our poor old dinghy, which was swirling around in the backwash. A few more drenchings and we dragged her up high and dry. The surf had not damaged her beyond springing a plank and breaking the gunwale. This could easily be repaired, even by such unskilful carpenters as ourselves.

We swam out for the oars and then, at Cooknell's invitation, trooped up the beach to a little coconut grove on the edge of the jungle, close to a gurgling stream which came down from the hills. The water from this stream was beautifully fresh and, in spite of the tropical heat, ice-cold. In this shady grove Gooknell, who told us he was an Englishman from Coventry, had built a rough shelter from an old sail. He had arrived in the black schooner, *Franklin Barnett*, but hastened to explain that he did not get on very well with the rest of the party, who were working on the hilltop.

"I've found the treasure," he said. "I'm only two feet from it and if you fellows help me to dig the rest of the dirt away I'll give you a share."

I looked at Bully for inspiration to frame a reply. Bully's face remained like a stone. We did not know what to say. That a man should offer to share a treasure of gold with two strangers for the digging of two foot of soil was beyond our comprehension. So to break the silence which followed this amazing offer Bully mumbled in a half-hearted fashion: "Sure. We'll help."

Cooknell said no more about it and proceeded to cook a dinner. We assured him that we had plenty of stores on board and warned him not to run himself short for the mere courtesy of inviting us to a meal. But he would not hear of it.

"I've got a booby bird and some rice," he said, "but it will take a long time to cook."

These booby birds are the easiest things in the world to catch. They will perch on a boat or on branches ashore and show no fear of mankind. We soon learned to approach them with a heavy stick, pick out the likeliest-looking of the bunch, and clout him over the head. The others would not make any attempt to fly away and would regard the murder of their comrade with a quaint cock of the head. The breast, legs and liver need a deal of cooking, some three hours or more, but are palatable and nourishing, if a bit tough at times. And a good broth can be made with the addition of a little flour and a few onions.

So our host, with a hand shaking violently from years of sleepy sickness, lit a primus stove and put on the pot. While the cooking was in progress we went for a swim. The three of us stripped naked and jumped into the breakers. For Bully and me, after twenty-seven grimy days at sea, it was a glorious refresher. We could ride the surf in to the beach, dive below the breakers and come up after they had swept by. And all the time each of us kept a wary eye open for sharks. Only fifty yards away they went up and down like Palace guards, but never did they venture inside the line of the breakers.

The meal was good. A pleasant change from our sea diet. A pipe of tobacco, and we sat and yarned until evening. We wanted to know all about the island, the people on the hill and the schooner. Gooknell spoke of his fellow inhabitants with something approaching disgust. We gathered that there was already a war of sorts going on on this desert isle.

Apparently on the hill there lived a man shrouded in mystery. He was master of the *Franklin Barnett* and son of an old man who was confined entirely aboard the schooner. We had given the schooner a hail before coming ashore but, receiving no reply, we had presumed her crew to be ashore. However, Cooknell assured us that the old man was probably asleep below.

The captain's name, we were told, was Ronald Valentine, and he had been living on the hill for several months. Cooknell was a passenger from Balboa in the schooner and had requested to be left ashore because he was confident that his metal divining powers would result in his locating the treasure.

With the help of her auxiliary engine, the *Franklin Barnett* had taken twenty-one days to make Cocos from Balboa and, so far as I could make out, Cooknell and Valentine had occupied themselves in a twenty-one-day squabble which only ceased when they parted company ashore.

Valentine's activities on the hill had us guessing. Cooknell said he was digging for treasure. Later we heard that he was an archaeologist hunting for specimens. A third theory was that he had come to Cocos for the purpose of investigating the conveyance of spiritual messages between Earth and the Beyond.

He apparently claimed to be a voice medium. Cooknell treated all these stories as "baloney" and maintained that Valentine had come simply to look for treasure and couldn't find any.

"Anyway," he added, "I've found the treasure, so he can dig holes in the hill till he's blue in the face."

An hour before sundown we heard voices coming down the hill.

"That's Sam and Harold Braun," explained Cooknell. "They sleep aboard the schooner and go up there to dig in the day."

Soon a black man broke through the bushes and dumped a water cask and haversack on the ground.

"Well, Mister Cooknell. You sure got visitors today." And turning to Bully and me he said: "I'm sure pleased to meet you, gentlemen. I see your little sloop from the hill."

Just then a young white man appeared, similarly laden and looking very tired. He was the white man we had seen from the boat on our arrival. He turned out to be a German-American from Chicago. Fed up with being a dishwasher, he had shipped aboard a fishing vessel which, although American owned, sailed from Los Angeles under the Panamanian flag. She had fished around the Galapagos and one night had come to anchor off Chatham Bay.

Braun, sick of the life and the perpetual diet of beans, jumped overboard as the vessel got under way at night. He could not swim, but had taken care to arm himself with a lifebelt and a piece of wood with which he hoped to paddle himself to the beach. But being much of a landsman he had not reckoned on the current setting him to the north-east and had drifted across the bay towards Nuez, with the cheerful prospect of missing the land altogether and being carried out to sea.

Just as he was being swept past a rocky projection he had paddled furiously and had managed to grab something solid ashore. He gasped as a thousand prickles stuck in his hand—he had got hold of a sea porcupine. But Braun knew better than to let go. He just had to hang on until he could get a foothold to drag himself up and ashore to safety.

The fishing vessel came back to look for him when they discovered that he was missing, and, after a fruitless search, gave him up for dead and steamed away. For two days Braun had remained in hiding in the jungle without food or water and at last, when the fishermen had gone away, he had given himself up to the mercies of Valentine and his companions. Valentine took pity on him and set him to work digging a huge shaft on the top of the hill. Braun dug while Sam wheeled the dirt away to the slope and shot it down.

Suffering from some stomach complaint and being unable to eat properly, Braun suffered agony as he laboured in the heat of the day. Being an unassuming young man with little confidence in himself, he had soon become a lackey and permitted himself to be cursed and shouted at by the domineering Sam.

Braun drawled a greeting to us and went off to wash himself in the stream. Sam did the talking. We helped them to get through the surf in their cockleshell boat, one that Sam had built himself and which was even more unstable than ours. Soon we followed, and after being thrown back on the beach three times, we got clear and repaired on board for supper.

Late that night Braun came alongside in a cayuca. He seemed unable to explain the reason for his visit, so we invited him aboard to eat. This he refused, but he sat watching us as we gulped the steaming hash. It seemed that he had something to say and could not bring himself to say it.

I asked him how long Valentine intended staying on the island. Braun fervently wished that it would not be long. He was tired of this everlasting dig, dig, dig; of carrying water up that killing hill trail like a pack horse; of being treated with contempt by Valentine and Sam. I expected a pleading request to let him come with us, but apparently he could not take courage enough to ask us straight Out and waited for the offer of a passage. This was not forthcoming.

There was a lot more umming and ahing and at last, having assured us that "he was sure glad to meet some fresh guys," he took his leave and went back to the schooner.

His visit set me thinking. There was trouble brewing on peaceful Cocos.

Next day we started on the heartbreaking business of watering ship. The usual hurly-burly in the surf was a thousand times worse when trying to get offshore with a cask of water. Three days we laboured before all the tanks were full. In the evenings we would sit in Cooknell's hut and yarn, sing or play poker. The poker games were for matches, which on Cocos were considerably more valuable than money. And so poor a player was I that I lost 870 matches in one night, but luckily Bully retrieved some by a bit of wild betting and prevented our stock from running too low.

Cooknell took us to where he was digging for treasure and Bully even threw some dirt about for the sake of a little exercise. But it was hot work with pick and spade, and he was soon back in the sea for a swim. In fact during the whole time we were on the island Cooknell made little effort to unearth "the extra two feet" which he said would reveal the treasure. Nor did we press him to do so, for the bushes were thick with millions of red ants which bit into our skin and produced terrible itching for something like half an hour. It was almost unbearable, and not even a bath in a cold stream would reduce the irritation.

Cooknell told us something of the visit of the *Avance.* She had left a few days before our arrival with a serious stretcher case on board. One of the principal members of the expedition, who was possessed of the strange name of Om Smith, fell down a sixty-foot waterfall on the south side of the island and fractured his hip. Two of the crew cut their way across the island to get help from the *Avance*, which was lying in Wafer Bay. It was only with great pain to the unfortunate Smith that he was eventually got on board, and the *Avance* left immediately for Balboa.

Cooknell had a hunch that Captain Stanton had left some men in Wafer Bay, and Braun and Sam also believed that there was someone there. There had been ructions among the crew, and from what I could make out some of them would be only too glad to remain ashore, even on Cocos. So we decided to go overland to find out. Cooknell said he would accompany us.

In the morning we hove up *Thelma*'s anchor to make sure that the chain had not taken a turn round the upper fluke, and dropped it again in the same place. So firmly did the anchor embed itself in the sand that I felt quite sure that it would be safe to leave the vessel for a short time. We took ashore two machetes, some ship's biscuits, the Webley automatic and a small camera. Cooknell was to provide a large tin of corned beef. We decided that since the island was interwoven with numerous fresh-water streams we would chance coming upon one of them rather than be burdened with water bottles. I arranged with Sam to wind the chronometer and feed the cat in the morning.

In the late afternoon, when the sun was low and the heat of the day over, we set out to climb the rocks on the far side of the bay and break our way into the jungle.

Disaster at Cocos

Our ascent of the rocks was a precarious business. Like flies we crawled and swarmed, with the surf thundering below us. The only footholds were small branches which every now and then broke away from under us, leaving a pair of kicking legs and a struggling body, suspended by one hand from an equally unreliable branch above. At last we scrambled up into the woods. The pocket compass was brought out to lay off the course. Gooknell took the lead, and off we went.

For a time it was easy going, at least easier than we expected. The way was clear and we were able to skirt round the steepest of the slopes. But there was one ridge which we could not circumvent, and so after half an hour's struggle three very leg-weary young men sat down at the top and consulted the compass for the next move.

Our way lay across a valley so dense with undergrowth that we could not tell how deep it was from above. The sides were so

precipitous that we could not find a way of getting down, and
tried to work round the edge. The jungle grew thicker and
thicker. Vines caught us by the feet and wound themselves round
our bodies; red ants attacked us continuously so that we were for
ever stopping to scratch furiously. It was hack, hack, all the time
with the machetes. We took it in turn to lead, for the man in front
had the worst of the cutting to do. Time and time again we would
come to a dead drop of two hundred feet or more and have to
retrace our steps to find somewhere else.

Once we came across a huge shaft in the side of a hill.
Cooknell said that this was dug by the Jolly expedition, which
came to the island in the old Brixham trawler *Vigilant.* The brink
of the shaft was overgrown and we might easily have fallen
down it and broken our necks had not Bully spotted it in time. As
we peered down I thought how amazing it was that a fairy tale fit
for nothing but a child's nursery book should make grown men
labour and sweat in such a God-forsaken spot. I wondered what
Cooknell's real thoughts were as he surveyed this work of
futility; if his confidence in his own little hole by Chatham Bay
was at all shaken.

Leaving Jolly's digging, we made another attempt to get
round the valley, and at last were lucky enough to find a place
where we could hold on to some branches and swing ourselves
across a ravine. More hacking and cutting, our clothes torn and
tattered, our skin itching and bleeding. Gooknell, with his long
hair and beard, looked like a caveman as he wielded his machete
to the accompaniment of Bully's flaming language. In fact
between the three of us we said so much about the jungle of
Cocos Island that we almost burnt a trail before us.

Just before sundown we came upon a pig trail which led us
approximately in the right direction. Following the footsteps of a
pig is no easy matter, for he is inclined to run along the edge of a
precipice in a hair-raising manner, but at least we found our
progress a little more rapid, even though it often meant crawling
along on our hands and knees. It has been reported in the past
that there is a species of snake on Cocos Island, but we trusted
our safety to the assumption that all snakes would have been
exterminated by the pigs. Snakes cannot live where pigs abound.

Darkness came with the usual tropical suddenness. The sun

went down, so fast that we almost fancied we could hear it drop, and left us clinging to the side of a bush-grown hill. We had already cast about in vain for a place to camp, so we decided just to lie down where we were and await the dawn.

I shall never forget that night in the jungle. Between sessions of scratching red ants, we ate a frugal meal of biscuits and corned beef, saving a few biscuits for the morrow. We were thirsty, too, after our trail cutting efforts, but this we had to suffer in silence for we had not struck a single stream since leaving the coast.

We sang a song or two for the sake of something to do, raising our croaking voices to the amazement of the wild life around us. The darkness was so impenetrable that we could not see more than a few feet. Every now and then queer noises pierced the silence; a bird would squawk in a treetop; a pig would go crashing by, sending a shower of dirt down the backs of our necks as we lay down trying to sleep. And from somewhere below us came the dull rumble of the surf.

Tired out, we did not have any trouble dropping off to sleep. Digging our heels into the earth to prevent ourselves slipping down the slope, we dozed off like babes in the woods. I dreamed I was in heaven, playing poker with Gooknell, who appeared to me in the guise of a clergyman sitting on a golden stool.

After about half an hour I awoke to the rustling of the trees. Cooknell was already sitting up.

"Squall coming."

I noticed the direction of the wind and felt thankful to find it westerly, for *Thelma* would be protected by the lee of the land. The wind swished through the treetops, the vines waved mystically about us. Birds clucked and fluttered. Then down came the rain.

As Bully said, it was more like lead shot than rain. There was no shelter from it. It soaked us through and stung our bodies so that we huddled together for the sake of mutual protection. Within ten minutes it was all over, but the damage was done. The ground beneath us was soaked. Water from the leaves continued to drip on us if to prolong the discomfort. A bird dropping landed in Cooknell's face; a heavy piece of dead wood, broken off by the wind, fell from a tree and hit me in the back; Bully had another attack of red ants.

We beat our hands and arms to try to keep warm and, failing to do so, I got up and groped about for firewood. Here and there I found a dry piece which I threw to Gooknell, who piled them under a fallen trunk. Several attempts to get a fire going failed because of damp matches and damp wood. At last a little flame flickered up. I heaved more dead vines on to it. The flicker turned to a blaze.

We might easily have set fire to the whole jungle, but we were not in the mood to care whether we did or not. We stood round and dried our clothes. Bully was soon asleep again. I have never seen a man with such a capacity for sleep, even under the most unconducive conditions. To him a plank is as good as a feather bed. I have even known him fall asleep while walking on his beat down a street in Edmonton. He only woke up when he hit the pavement and saw his helmet rolling along the gutter. Kind passers-by thought he had fainted. One of these days he'll go to sleep while he's having a swim. I guess that would be a good long snooze!

Gooknell lay back once more and put his hat over his face to defy the marksmanship of the bird above. I listened for a time to all those eerie noises which one only hears at night in a tropical jungle before I, too, fell fast asleep. We had agreed to watch the fire in turns.

Hardly had I slumbered than I was awakened again by something cold running down my chest. More rain.

Down it came. The fire went out. Our dried clothes became wringing wet again. Once more our skins turned to gooseflesh. A squelching mud came through the bed of ferns we were lying on. In despair we moved a little higher. up the hill. There was a dryish patch beneath an overhanging bush. We crawled under and lay down again.

Cooknell and Bully snatched a few odd moments' sleep. I gave it up and just waited for the first signs of daylight. The hours seemed endless. At last a faint streak appeared through the trees. I woke the other two and we gathered up our belongings to begin all over again before the sun came over the horizon.

Hack, hack, hack. We stumbled across a litter of pigs. Their mother led them off at a wild scamper and it was no use shooting, for we could neither have cooked the pork nor carried it. And for myself, I hadn't the heart to shoot a baby pig, however hungry I might have been.

So on we went, climbing, stumbling and sliding. None of us would admit that we were on the verge of collapse, and no one cared to show so much weakness as to suggest a rest so early in the day. We often laughed over it afterwards, for when the journey was over we each admitted that we were praying for someone to call a halt. Twice we found ourselves ascended to dizzy heights from where we could overlook Chatham Bay. Twice we were forced round in a circle and came back to the same place. We could see a great mountain not far away.

At last we reached the end of the uphill part of our journey. All the land below us was of a lower level, and with lighter hearts we started on a grand slide, hoping to goodness we would soon find a drinking place. Down we went, slithering and sliding, dislodging stones and boulders, on our way. Often we slid long distances on our backsides as it was too steep to stand up.

Once I slithered some two hundred feet with a big boulder rumbling down a few yards behind me. The boulder and I were both going at the same speed. I tried to get out of its way but the damned thing seemed to persist in following me. Suddenly I came to a dead drop of some twenty feet. I crashed down into the ferns and bushes beneath. The boulder flew over my head and went thundering down towards the sea.

For an hour we continued our hectic descent. Bully had started out wearing a pair of heavy American Army boots. Before we reached the other end of that slide the heels were gone and the backs were worn clean off. Only the toes and uppers remained.

Once we came across some marks on the trees where the Leckie expedition of some years before had blazed a trail. But all other signs of the trail were obliterated. It was in the settlement which Leckie's men had built on the beach at Wafer Bay that we hoped to find some men from the *Avance*.

Soon the beach came into view and we saw two crazy huts of corrugated iron below us. We shouted and fired pistol shots in the air. No reply. Not a sign of life. Our hearts sank. Had we endured all this for nothing?

In a few minutes we landed in a swampy vale and tramped out

to the sea shore. A short walk along the beach and we came to
the first hut. All that remained of it was the roof and two sides.
The back and front had disappeared. The floor had been torn up
for firewood. The only sign that it had once been inhabited was a
painted notice on a coconut tree nearby: "Vive Le Costa Rica."

We dragged our weary feet a little further to where a stream
ran out into the bay. We lay on our bellies for a long-delayed
drink. The water was not so good as at Chatham Bay. It tasted of
mud and dead wood. So busy were we in satisfying our thirst that
we did not look into the second hut until we heard a shout. Who
should come striding down the sand but the giant Sinsbury, not a
stitch of clothing on his huge body. Close behind came the burly
Burwood.

There were hearty handshakes and greetings. It's good to
meet old friends on a place like Cocos. The preliminaries over,
our first thought was for food.

"How do you go for stores?"

"We've got enough to last us a month. We're hoping the
Avance will be back by then. Harold and I volunteered to stay
behind."

There came a sumptuous meal of wheat cakes. Burwood and
Sinsbury lived almost entirely on wheat, which they ground up in
an old coffee grinder. Cooknell was fanciful enough to point out
the weevils in his grub instead of eating it quickly in the
approved fashion. Bully swore it was the finest meal he had ever
gobbled down. For myself I was so fatigued that I lay on our
hosts' bunk, protected by mosquito nets, which had holes in them
big enough to admit a seagull, and fell into a deep sleep for two
hours.

They had a comfortable little cubbyhole. Sinsbury had been a
carpenter by trade and saw to it that there was a table and two
chairs, made from crazy-shaped branches.

I noticed that Cooknell was somewhat coolly received.
Apparently he had been one of the originators of the *Avance*
expedition and, after cutting adrift from the rest of the party at
the start, beat them to it and arrived on Cocos first. The
atmosphere of desolation on the island did not seem to help them
to forget their differences. In fact the island seemed to breed
discontent. Even Burwood and Sinsbury were harsh and bitter

with one another, constantly quarrelling and bickering in a manner which struck us as childish as well as inconsiderate. It was a case of two men, entirely unsuited for each other's company, being thrown together by fate and becoming sick to death of the sight of each other.

Sinsbury could sing. He had a beautiful voice and was wont to burst into song on every possible occasion. Personally I liked to listen to him, but Burwood had had enough of it. He raved and swore at every note and constantly implored his companion to "Shut up for Christ's sake." This annoyed Sinsbury, and he sang all the more.

The island was, at the time, inhabited by six people, excluding ourselves. And among those six there were three feuds waging continuously,

Valentine   v.   Cooknell
Cooknell   v.   Sinsbury and Burwood
Sinsbury   v.   Burwood.

Valentine and Cooknell, camping within a quarter of a mile of each other, were not even on speaking terms. Cooknell refused to share the more comfortable quarters at Wafer Bay with Sinsbury and Burwood. Sinsbury and Burwood said they wouldn't have him anyway. And the unpleasantness dragged on and on — an absurd state of affairs for a party of grown men lumped together on a desert island.

However, Bully and I would have no part in it. We refused to be drawn into disagreements of any kind and hoped to heaven that this wrangling fever would not prove contagious and affect our own relationship. We sat on the floor in the evening and had a sing-song before rolling over for the sleep of the just. Sinsbury and I, taking a couple of rifles (they had a veritable arsenal at Wafer Bay), rose early and trudged off to hunt a pig. After an hour of scrambling about in the undergrowth, which was too much like the journey of the day before for my liking, we gave it up and returned to a breakfast of wheat cakes.

The *Avance* had left her lifeboat at Wafer Bay and Burwood and Sinsbury having caulked and painted it, we all agreed to row round to Chatham Bay. Cooknell, Bully and I had had our fill of jungle cutting. The Wafer Bay pair said they would be glad of the trip to break the monotony of their existence.

So off we went, taking it in turns with the big oars and passing between Nuez and the main island. It was hard work punching the current, and several times we struck up a shanty to urge our aching limbs.

I was glad to be on my way back. A cloud of depression seemed to be hanging over me all the time at Wafer Bay. While the others scampered in and out of the water and played golf on the beach with a round stone and a crooked branch, I could only sit around and mope. I must have been dull company.

I thought it was sheer tiredness after our efforts in the jungle, but as things turned out it was that vague mental warning to which the human mind is sometimes subjected when something dreadful is going to happen.

At last we got Nuez astern and bore away to cross Chatham Bay. Soon we could see the masts of the *Franklin Barnett*, and as it was not so easy to see her against the background of jungle on the far side of the bay I felt no qualms at not sighting *Thelma*'s stumpy stick straight away. But as we grew closer I stood up in the prow and scanned the bay. *Thelma* was not there!

Wild thoughts ran through my head. I at first imagined that Braun and Sam had seized her and sailed away, leaving their taskmaster on the island. It was known that, apart from the hatred they had for each other, they were discontented with the shortage of food in the schooner and had said more than enough to show that they would be glad to get away from the island.

Then, far away in a corner of the bay, I caught sight of her. She was but a few yards from the rocks. Even as I watched a huge wave lifted her up and carried her in.

We rowed like fiends, but the tide and current were against us. I stood there and saw her rise again and disappear. When the next breaker came she did not come up. She was down on her beam ends with the surf pounding over her.

Sam and Braun appeared from the beach, rowing frantically to the scene of the disaster. Before we got there they had reached the wreck and were off with a boat load of gear. It turned out that they had saved my sextant, the chronometer and some tinned food.

There was very little wind but it was, impossible to get the lifeboat alongside in the breakers. We anchored a little way off and veered down as near as possible. The sight before us almost broke my heart. There was the gallant little vessel, which I had loved and cared for all these years, which had brought us safely through fair weather and foul for nearly 7,000 miles on this cruise alone, in her death throes on that lonely shore. All our worldly belongings danced and swirled among the rocks. A bunch of dollar notes washed by us to disappear in the foam. Pieces of timber floated everywhere.

It was enough to chill the heart of the bravest soul. To complete the mournful scene Jimmy, drenched and scared, meowed pitifully from the masthead.

Salvage Work

Sam and Braun arrived on the scene again and Gooknell and I jumped into their crazy boat and scrambled aboard *Thelma*.

"I think we can save her yet," yelled Sam above the thunder of the surf. I took one look at the way she lay and knew that the vessel was doomed.

She hardly rose an inch to a breaking wave, and there was a sickening grinding and snapping of timbers with each cruel blow. Every wave broke clean over her and forced us to cling on for our lives.

We fought our way down into the tiny cabin. Each wave filled her up and we were imprisoned like rats until it subsided. We choked and gasped as we grabbed such things as were within reach and passed them out on deck. Sam worked like a hero. It was impossible to stay below for long at a time and the negro, still convinced that the vessel could be saved, rowed off to the schooner with Bully and the rest to fetch a big anchor and chain. I very much admired his optimism. As I struggled in the cabin I could feel the rocks under my feet. The whole of her starboard side was ripped out. Something was sticking up through the cabin floor.

There was nothing to be done except to try to save everything possible. Jimmy was escorted to the shore, but unfortunately as

Burwood held her in his arms to jump ashore the lifeboat overturned. Still holding on to the cat, he dived to escape being crowned by the boat. When he came up in shallow water Jimmy was struggling and biting in his arms, having clawed a beautiful map of the Panama railroad on her rescuer's chest.

It was about 2p.m. when the *Thelma* was wrecked, and we had to race against sundown to get the most important valuables ashore. I cut off the mainsail, threw out such tinned food as I could find and handed it up to Cooknell. The others, seeing the futility of laying out the schooner's anchor, formed a human chain over the rocks and passed the goods up to a place above high water mark. As the tide ebbed and left the vessel clear of the breakers we got off the spars and heavy gear and stripped her of everything which might be washed away on the next tide.

Well into the night we worked, not a man of us saving himself the slightest effort. Sam, who was a lover of boats and had often expressed his liking for *Thelma*, realised our distress to the full. We would have cared little for the loss of our money and belongings had we been able to save the ship. He expressed himself in his strange, individual style as we laboured under our loads.

"I know what it is, Captain Roberts," (he always called me Captain Roberts, although I had then not the slightest claim to the title). "I know what it is to lose a ship. I'm a seaman."

I thanked him for his unselfish assistance and promised him some reward.

"I don't want no reward, Captain Roberts. I'm a seaman. You're a seaman. It's my duty to help you."

Sam had his faults, but I liked him for those words.

That night we all went aboard the schooner for a few hours' rest. We were greeted by an aged person, stark naked. He was sunburned a rich brown and looked as healthy as ever a man of sixty-five could be. There was not an ounce of superfluous flesh on him, though this, I learned, was in great part due to the lack of stores aboard the ship.

This was Valentine Senior. A proud old Pennsylvanian of English descent. Soldier, traveller, adventurer, author— he had been everything and had wandered far, filling his years to the very hour.

Charming and courteous, he made shift to give us such
comforts as were possible, even to offering his bunk to one of us,
which of course we indignantly refused. To distinguish him from
his son we called him Old Man Valentine, though not at all with
any feeling of disrespect.

The quarrel fever of Cocos had not failed to run riot in the
schooner, for apart from the friction between Sam and Braun,
Sam and O.M.V. hated each other more and more every day.

We were up before dawn to carry on the work of salvage
while Sam and Braun returned to. their digging on the hill. At
low water *Thelma* was almost high and dry and I was able to
discover the cause of the wreck. Trailing from her bow were
many fathoms of anchor chain but no anchor. One of the links
had been sawn clean through as if with a file. It was the work of
the mushroom coral. So sharp was the edge of it that in five days
it had cut through a heavy link as the vessel swung gently to her
hawse. I should never have believed that coral could cut through
solid iron so efficiently. Later we found pieces on the beach
which would file through any iron or steel we possessed. But the
knowledge came too late. The worst was done. Some time after
the wreck we found that anchor still firmly embedded in the sand
and it took four of us to weigh it from the lifeboat.

All the gear deposited above high water mark had to be
carried over rocks to the beach, about a quarter of a mile away.
We had no boots or shoes and, barefooted, we took a lot of
punishment. On the day before, when I was down in the cabin, I
had been knocked down by a wave and had broken a toe. This
hindered me all the more, but Bully was also badly cut and
bruised before the day was very old.

O.M.V. insisted on coming ashore to give us a hands though
we felt guilty for allowing a man of his age to take part in such
gruelling labour. It was no use taking light loads; we would never
have finished the task. It was a case of humping as much stuff on
our backs as we could withstand and then struggling over the
slippery rocks as best we could.

From all that we possessed and valued in the world we saved:

Shotgun and pistol (not on board at the time of the wreck)	
Camera	Squaresail yard
A spare anchor	Box full of blocks
All our sails	Thirty fathoms of warp
Sextant	Sheets and halliards
Tin of tobacco	Boom and gaff
Two five-gallon tins of petrol	Box of books and charts
A dollar note	Forty tins of corned beef
Two log books	Primus stove
Ensign and Burgee	

Every article, especially the sails and rope, seemed to be twice its weight as we tried to jump from rock to rock, and it was not until four days later that we dumped the last of it on the beach near Cooknell's shelter. The chronometer and watch were found to be full of sea-water and in a hopeless condition.

At the first opportunity I climbed the hill trail to see the mysterious Captain Valentine to thank him for sending his men down to help. He could not come himself for I learned that he had only one leg — and a steep jungle trail with a wooden leg is no light matter.

While I was yet puffing and blowing I came upon this man of whom I had heard so much. My first impression was the reincarnation of Sir Francis Drake. Sitting before a tent, his wooden leg stretched out before him, he was smoking his pipe and reading a book. I noticed that the book was on spiritualism.

He affected a small, pointed beard, wore a French beret and was stripped to the waist. I bade him not to rise as I approached, out of consideration for his physical disability, but could see as he sat that he was a finely-built man, broad of shoulder and some six feet or more in height. An impressive figure, and one which for a time held me in interest and fascination.

The preliminaries over, he expressed his sympathy for the loss of *Thelma* and laid himself out to entertain the rest of the party, who, bar Cooknell, had followed me up the hill. He talked of his work on the hill as an archaeologist, and of the wonderful specimens of rock he had discovered, always keeping us guessing as to why he should have come to Cocos for these samples rather than to the islands nearer the mainland.

He spoke of his "great work", which he seemed reluctant to define, and of his familiarity with the spirits of the dead. He claimed to be a voice medium, and said that during his lonely nights on the hill he often sat and talked with spirit friends who had "passed over." In fact I judged that he would have something to reveal on the theory of spiritualism when he returned to civilisation.

He talked of Cooknell, of what he called the Englishman's unfortunate disposition, and laughed at his prospects of finding treasure down on the beach. At no time did Valentine suggest that he himself had come to Cocos for treasure, though it looked mighty like it the way Braun and Sam were digging away in a huge pit close by. I noticed, too, that on the captain's table was a piece of wire shaped like a cross such as gold diviners use. Cooknell also had one.

So, all in all, I knew not what to make of the man — archaeologist, spiritualist or treasure hunter? But he talked so much that I started to lose concentration and my thoughts began to wander so that it was hard put to bring myself back to pick up the flow of his talk.

An hour or more we were there, and Burwood and Sinsbury showed keen interest in our host's spiritual preaching. They, also, believed that the spirit within a man cannot die and that it is only the body which decays.

Valentine wound up by assuring us that he would be only too glad to take us back to Balboa in the *Franklin Barnett*, although the uncertainty of his work prevented him from naming a date of sailing. It would have to be soon, for they were already in need of stores and were living chiefly on beans.

"But whatever we've got," he said, slapping me on the shoulder, "you're welcome to a share of it."

And for that I liked him better, for it seemed to come from his heart more than all that he had said in the last hour.

So Bully and I hobbled off down the trail to resume our labours, leaving the others as an audience for the captain. Cooknell had a dinner ready for us and offered his assistance in the pitching of a camp close to his own shelter. I will say of Cooknell that he sweated a great deal more than he need have done to help us out of our troubles. He never picked a light load when coming over the rocks with the salvage, and I was amazed at his muscular strength. Slightly built, with narrow, drooping shoulders, he gave the impression of extreme delicacy, especially with the constant trembling which afflicted him. But there was no denying that he could lift as much, if not more, than either one of us. And many were the tricks of agility and contortion he could perform on the sands which had us beaten as soon as we tried to copy him.

In his days of farming in Australia, he told us, the old hands used to sit around the camp fire at night and lay bets on the tricks and trials of strength between the youngsters. Cooknell being of anything but robust appearance, the odds were always against him, and he won much silver for those who knew of his accomplishments. I, too, would back him against many a trickster I have paid to see.

We built a tent with our squaresail for a roof and a pile of stones as the floor: it looked a cosy enough place from afar but it was the very devil to sleep in. We did not care to level the floor with sand because the beach was full of fleas, so a sail spread on the hard uneven floor was the best bed we could devise. How we envied Cooknell his camp bed and his blankets!

Sleeping we found very difficult after our berths aboard *Thelma.* The nights on Cocos were sometimes remarkably cold in comparison with the heat of the day, and we found little warmth sleeping beneath a couple of jibs. The red ants swarmed beneath our bedding and attacked us with such ferocity that we would leap up in a frenzy of scratching. The itching would give way to the mosquitoes' drone. We covered our heads with canvas to keep them out, but once inside they were likely to drive a man insane. So up again and shake them out. What with these creatures, the sand flies and the land crabs we found a stone bed on a tropical island to be not nearly so comfortable as life at home. But we had chosen to get out of the rut of everyday life, so we had to sleep in the bed we had made as best we could.

In the mornings we would hunt for pigs in the woods, jump in the surf for a cooler and bag a booby bird or two for dinner. We found it economical to share our food with Cooknell, for the mutual saving of fuel for the stove. Cooknell was a great hand at devising new dishes and, Bully and I having exhausted our ideas at sea, he did more than his share of galley work.

Sinsbury and Burwood returned in their boat to Wafer Bay. Apart from the fact that they could not bear Cooknell's company, nor Cooknell theirs, there was not enough to feed five men on the limited supplies at Chatham Bay. The few tins we had salvaged would not last long, even when supplemented by booby birds and Cooknell's stock of Navy beans.

One afternoon Cooknell said he felt it in his bones that a ship would come that day. Sure enough, at about five o'clock in the evening, a steamship suddenly appeared round the north-eastern point of the island. I believe she was flying the British flag, but the vessel was too far off to distinguish it with any degree of accuracy. She had only one funnel, red with a black top. To this day I do not know what ship she was so far from the usual steamer lanes. She came so slowly across the mouth of Chatham Bay that we thought she was going to anchor, and jumped for joy in anticipation of a decent dinner: but to our dismay she proceeded on her way and disappeared round Nuez Island.

A few days later Burwood and Sinsbury came back to take O.M.V. round to their camp. They, too, had seen the steamer but said she did not stop in Wafer Bay.

The old man was virtually a prisoner in the schooner and was delighted at the prospect of a break in his monotonous existence afloat. Bully went with them. I chose to stay behind, for there are times when I find solace in loneliness. I continued to take my meals with Cooknell and went my own way for the rest of the day.

I chiselled the name of *Thelma* on a huge rock, and as I tapped away little canaries came and sat around with an air of curiosity, quite unafraid. If I stopped tapping they all flew away, but no sooner did I start again than they would be all about me like flies. The tap, tap, tap seemed to fascinate them.

Many an hour I spent wandering along the beach reading the names carved on the rocks. Here and there I found the name of a ship I knew or had read of. Some were very old and upside down, where the land had fallen into the sea. The older ones, over a hundred years old, were mostly of the old whaling vessels which used to come into the North Pacific every year and would call at Cocos for water. In some places men had carved their own names and the date; and who knows but that, in some cases, this rough lettering was their last living record. Voyages were long in those days, spreading over years, and navigation was fraught with many more dangers than today. So these names may be of vital interest to the descendants of those early seafarers. For this reason I wrote down every name, ship or man, that I could find, and list them here. Many more there were, but so regularly washed by the sea that the words were no longer legible.

Thelma (E.Y.C.) London	1934
Yacht *Mary Pinchot*	1929(and the names of the crew)
Mariposa	1869-1870
Mariposa	Oct. 17, 1871
Jose R. Quiros	1927
Costa Rica II	April 5, 1933
Sloop *Driftwood*	1933
U.S.S. *Sacramento*	28th Oct, 1931
Engla	1849
J. Baleana	1814
Martha, Newport, 0. Potter	1839
Dexter	1846
J. Maria, Zeledon Julio	22, 1819
C. Marks	1871
Virginia Marks	April 11th
ship *Uncas*, H. C. Bunker, Falmouth	1933
ship *Kingston*	August, 1834
S. Spearman	1888
Vagabondia	1931
Yetara	1926-28
S.Y. *Queen of Scots*	Mar, 1929
Nahlin R.T.Y.C.	1931
Arcadia	4—'29
Turr. Dalb.	1895
O.L.P.	1931
Haida	1931
Camargo	1930-31
Sloop *1 eddy*	5.1.1930
Ship *Nye*. E. Smith	1833
M.S. *Atlantic*	April 1930 (This was painted on a board with names of the crew, and nailed to a tree)
J. Sousa, S.D. Cal	1930 (Sousa was an Engineer in the m.s. *Atlantic*)

H. Craggs   1923
H.B.M. Steam Frigate *Sampson* 1847
C.P.T. Baley   1848
Bark *Cornelia*
Velero III
C. S. Ergonbroot   1856
Ship *Atala*. C. Winship, Boston, May 4, 1817
B. West   1830
J. Mitchell   1833
Ship *Brandley*   Feb. 1. 1842
Bark *Octatda*, C. Mantor
Ship *Ocean*   1853
Ship *Arrison* N. Bedford April 5, 1842
Bark *Ben*
Mary and Susan
C. Fay   1842
Nourma Hal'33(inland)
L. N. Smile   1833
B. B. Lamphier   1841
H. P. Wood   1915
H. C. Brown, Hull   1914
Yacht *Messinet*   1905
Sister Sue   1882
H. Kermak ————— 1828 (this name lies underwater at high
tide and is very indistinct but is followed by the letters K— — —
bhav — —)
W. Marshall, New York   1901
Sloop *Sunshine*   1871

Exploring Ashore

I determined one day that, the work of salvage being completed, I would see something of the interior. This in spite of our experiences on the trip to Wafer Bay. So before dawn the next morning I took my gun and knife and set off while Gooknell was yet asleep. This time I refused to burden myself with a machete, for the only hope I had of getting inland was to follow the course of one of the many streams.

Not far from the camp I found I was being followed by the faithful Jimmy, tail vertical and seemingly very pleased with her new surroundings. So she became my companion in the exploration.

I could not fail to pause in my climbing to look at the wonderful scenery of the jungle. Down through a vista of overhanging trees and wild rambling bushes, hanging vines and great grey boulders, there tumbled and splashed a gorgeous waterfall, sparkling in the morning sun. Here indeed was a glimpse of nature undefiled by the hand of man. The only sign of life was a wild cat which scampered off at my approach.

Thus encouraged, I climbed higher, jumping from rock to rock with the agile Jimmy at my heels. After two hours' travelling in this manner I came upon a deep ravine running to the eastward and fairly clear of bush. I took rough bearings of my position by the sun and trudged off into this great hollow of land. Pig tracks abounded and suddenly I came upon a full grown boar grubbing up roots. I dared not move lest he detect my presence. Only his broad, fat stern was visible. I levelled the gun and fired. A charge of buckshot flew into his posterior.

I had hoped to bring him down with a wound in the leg and then jump him; but before the report echoed back through the woods he was off like a streak of lightning. I never before saw a pig run so fast. Drawing my knife, I dropped the gun and careered after him. He zig-zagged and climbed until he had me pouring with perspiration; but I felt confident that I would catch him, for he was already starting to limp.

So the wild chase went on until the quarry made a sharp turn and started to climb out of the ravine. I hastened to cut him off, when suddenly my feet disappeared from under me and I descended into a world of darkness. For a moment I lost my wits, and it was some time before I realised that I was sitting at the bottom of an evil smelling hole with an army of red ants crawling down the back of my shirt. I saw that the hole was the work of a man with a spade. What I said about treasure hunters in general and the Cocos lot in particular was unrepeatable, but the idiot who dug that hole lost me my dinner and nearly broke my neck into the bargain. They ought to rename Cocos the Island of Holes. As I clambered out into the air again I felt that I would like to take by the scruff of the neck every man who had ever dug a hole on Cocos and make him fill it in again.

I looked round for Jimmy. She had disappeared. Feeling a little disgruntled and in some pain from my broken toe, I struggled back to where I had dropped the gun and commenced to wend my way back to camp, not a little worried over the vanishing of Jimmy.

I arrived back in time for a meal of fish which Sam had brought ashore for us, and was relieved to find Jimmy waiting patiently by Cooknell's side as he held the frying pan over the fire.

This brief excursion set me on edge to go again. A chart in Craggs' possession, dated 1795, showed a lake to be situated some little way inland. An account of the island, written in 1832, also refers to this lake; but no one in recent times has been able to find trace of it. It is reasonable to suppose that the numerous streams and cascades which decorate the island originate from some sort of reservoir, and possibly the existence of a lake of considerable size has more foundation than the likelihood of buried treasure. Cooknell, in spite of his long sojourn on the island, had never attempted to penetrate the interior, apart from our jaunt to Wafer Bay, and expressed a desire to accompany me the next day.

We were up betimes and well into the woods by daybreak and soon struck the waterfall I had seen the previous day. Following the course of the same stream we came upon a deep pool, some fifteen yards across and over six feet deep, for we could not touch the bottom with our feet. We swam around for a time, enjoying the invigorating coldness of the water. Nearby was a hollow in the land, the same level as the pool, and I thought that in the rainy season this might easily be flooded to form the lake shown on Craggs' chart. It was not far from the position indicated.

We were soon on our way again, but after a bit more climbing and walking Cooknell suggested that we return. He had had enough, he said. I would not hear of going back at this stage and Cooknell refused to go on. So we parted company, he calling me a bloody fool for going on and I repressing my anger for fear of causing ructions in the camp later on. After seeing the worthless quarrels of other people on the island I restrained from high words, turned my back on him and pressed on upstream.

A little further on I came upon evidence that I was not the only one to ascend this rockstrewn stream. Carved in a piece of soft stone was;

Nourma Hal, '33

This, I learned later, was the yacht belonging to Viscount Astor, the millionaire.

The going became more and more difficult. Insurmountable boulders blocked my path and often I had to leave the stream and push through the undergrowth. There were several more deep pools, like the first we found, any one of which might be turned into a lake by heavy rainfalls.

Everywhere there were signs of landslips, some obviously quite recent. And as a matter of small interest I found an army of ants using a spider's web to cross a stream. I supposed they had first killed the spider.

Passing through a deep and narrow cut in the hillside, walls of rock towering on either side and almost shutting out the light, I emerged on the other side to find a number of young coconut trees flourishing by the banks of a stream. There were more a little further on, but nowhere could I find an old or nut-bearing tree. It was therefore something of a mystery how these young trees had come to spring up, as they all appeared to be of about the same age. My conclusion was that they must have been planted, for indeed there was a distinct regularity about their spacing. But by whom?

On one occasion I left the water to cross a ridge where the undergrowth was least dense. My reason for doing this was that I observed a definite trail which appeared to be that of something much larger than a pig. Small trees and branches lay broken on either side of a beaten track.

I searched for signs of the hand of man. But there were none. It seemed that the bush had been trodden down some time before and the broken wood was already beginning to rot. I followed this trail as far as a patch of grass which would have made an ideal camping place had I wished to extend my explorations into the next day. I regretted not having brought stores and equipment to do so, but sat down instead and made careful note of all that I had seen. I also drew a rough chart of the course and distance I had made.

Having now lost sight of the stream, I proceeded in a north-easterly direction until I came to a clear valley, from where I could hear the burbling of water ahead. After twenty minutes struggling through vines I found myself once more by the stream,

not a little thankful, for I had had a fear of being bushed without
the water to guide me.

I covered another mile or so, climbing over the rocks, until
my way became so steep that I could not make much more than
fifty yards progress in half an hour. The stream divided into two,
and I rested on a stone to make a further estimate of my position.
I reckoned that I was somewhere between the two mountain
peaks, nearer the foot of the higher.

By this time I was tired and aching in every limb, and deemed
it wise to return lest I be caught by darkness as we had been
before. So, munching a piece of coconut I had brought with me, I
set out for Chatham Bay, satisfied with my day's outing but still
hoping to go even further afield before leaving the island.

The return journey was uneventful, apart from the fact that I
once lost my way for an hour and later took an unexpected
plunge, fully clothed and complete with gun and ammunition,
into one of the deep pools. In clambering round the precipitous
edge I missed my footing and dropped ten feet into the water
below. I took care to dry the ammunition in the sun, and the gun
did not seem to be in the least affected.

I arrived back at the camp well before sundown and found
Cooknell busy with the stewpot. We soon forgot the incident of
the morning and settled down to the everlasting game of poker
draw.

On the evening of the tenth day after the wreck a small steam
fishing vessel came round the point and anchored in the bay.
There was no peace for Braun until he had made out her name as
Reliance, Los Angeles, for he feared that it was his own vessel
returned. We waited in vain for them to lower a boat and come
ashore and at last Sam and Braun rowed off to the schooner. At
dawn the next morning the fishermen got under way again and
Sam came back to tell us that her skipper was Japanese.

"They ain't got no food nor nothin'," said the disconsolate
Sam, "just beans and flour, same as us."

I paid another visit to Captain Valentine, this time
accompanied by Cooknell. I had hoped that these two would
enter upon some form of reconciliation, but we had been on the
hill no longer than ten minutes before they were at loggerheads
again and cursing each other so that Cooknell stumped off down

the trail, leaving me with the irate skipper. When he had cooled
down he told me that he intended to sail on the evening of March
12th, and warned me to have all our belongings stowed on board
the schooner by that time.

Cooknell helped me fill all the fresh water tanks we had
salvaged, for I learned to my astonishment that the *Franklin
Barnett* only stowed 120 gallons. Bully, Sinsbury, Burwood and
O.M.V. returned from Wafer Bay and, with the help of the big
lifeboat, we got all the water and salvage aboard.

Bully and Sinsbury had been hunting and shot a pig. The four
legs they brought round to us. I asked Bully where the other parts
were. "We ate it," was the reply. "Harold Burwood is a
vegetarian, so Len and I knocked off eighteen chops between us.
He was only a skinny brute, and after all we had had enough
trouble carrying him home. We slung him on a pole and
staggered back with him like a couple of drunks. I fell down a
hole once and the pig slid down the pole and hit me on the back
of the head and nearly laid me out."

So we built a fire on the beach and each of us roasted a leg on
a stick. O.M.V., as well as Burwood, could not stomach pork, so
there was one whole leg for each of the rest of us. The art of
barbecue did not reveal itself in our efforts to make the pork
eatable, and in my case it was charcoal on the surface with raw
meat beneath. But as rations had been rather low it was a
welcome meal, in spite of the griping pains produced in the
stomach shortly afterwards.

That night, being the last we should have together on Cocos,
was celebrated by a sing-song after the feasting. Everybody gave
a song of some sort, even O.M.V. raising his voice in a catchy
American melody. Of course, Sinsbury was the star turn, in spite
of the disgust of his companion when he struck up "Sonny Boy."
Burwood was no mean singer either, and time and again we
called for his "Lyin' in the Hay."

It was with no small amount of sorrow that the merry party
broke up close on midnight. By the light of the moon we
launched the lifeboat through the surf and, with the exception of
Cooknell, rowed out to the schooner. There were good-byes to
Sinsbury and Burwood, for we were to sail next day, and they set
off for Wafer Bay.

The next day it was arranged for Bully and Braun to climb the hill and fetch down the captain's belongings while Sam and I got the schooner ready for sea. At first Sam attempted to order me about as he was accustomed to do with Braun, but I very soon put a stop to that in no uncertain manner.

As we went round the vessel reeving new halliards and greasing masts, I could see what a terrible condition she was in. Her mainmast was rotten at the hounds, so all her masthead gear was hung in rope slings to save any sudden strain. The rigging was slack and the steel screw boxes so rusted up that they were immovable. The rudder head was dangerously loose and her bottom so thick with huge barnacles that it was a wonder that she ever sailed at all. Big patches bare of paint showed along her water line and I had no doubt that in her planking was a populous colony of teredo worms.

She had been a fine vessel, built at Sheet Harbour, Nova Scotia, for the fishing fleet in 1911. She was sixty feet overall, with seven feet of normal draft and fifteen feet beam. There was an antiquated engine which, the skipper said, gave her seven knots in calm water. The main boom was rigged with lazy jacks, a handy American idea but unseamanlike to the old-fashioned British mind. The masts were stepped well forward, giving a huge main boom, the safety of which had to be cared for by a permanent preventer tackle.

Down below was a large cabin which had once been the fish hold, and there was a smaller cabin forward occupied by the old man. Sam slept aft with the Captain.

At last, when all was ready, I saw the figure of Captain Valentine hobbling down the hill trail. With his wooden leg it took him a long time to get to the bottom, but I saw him stump along the beach to Cooknell's shelter. What passed between them I do not know, but Cooknell preferred to stay on the island rather than to ship back in the *Franklin Barnett*.

What would happen to him I could not imagine, for I knew that when the *Avance* arrived he would not deign to ask for a passage with Stanton. So we left this lonely Englishman whose heart was so proud that he faced the dangers of starvation on that desolate place rather than take favours from people whom he regarded as his enemies. We left him our shotgun and such tinned supplies as we could spare from our much depleted store and set about getting the vessel to sea.

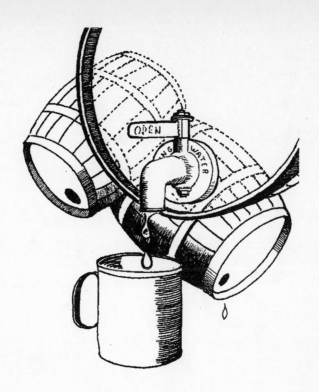

Farewell to Cocos

We manned the capstan and hove her short as evening closed
on the twelfth of March. The skipper took the wheel as we
paused in our labours on the foredeck.

"Break her out."

"Heave and she must. Come on now. Lend a hand, Braun."

Braun had never set foot aboard a sailing vessel before and
ran about like a lost sheep, wondering what all the ropes were for
and what the skipper meant by his orders.

Four of us threw our weight on the capstan bars, but not an
inch more anchor cable would come in over the bows. Neither
the kedge nor the bower would move, and there was a full hour's
cursing and sweating before a black mass showed itself above the
water. Both anchors were hopelessly mixed up with fathoms of
chain and seaweed twisted round them. Foot by foot we got **it**
clear, Sam going his own way about the job in open defiance of
the skipper's orders.

By the time the anchors were got on board the wind had fallen away and the schooner commenced to drift towards the rocks on which the bones of *Thelma* lay.

Without telling Valentine, for fear of his flying into a panic, Sam and I hastily dropped a kedge overboard on a warp to hold her while the others tried to start the engine. But the ancient engine refused to be started, and just as darkness closed about us a puff of wind came offshore and sent us out to the mouth of the bay.

It was not until we were well under way that we discovered what a narrow escape the schooner had had from a similar fate to my poor old *Thelma*. The great bower chain had been cut clean through just as ours had been, but luckily the loose end had got entangled with the upper fluke and had held the vessel from destruction. The kedge had been swinging clear of the bottom owing to the two chains becoming twisted. How long she had been lying like that we could not tell, for she had been at anchor in Chatham Bay for four and a half months.

Just as we were edging off the land a violent squall struck the vessel, accompanied by a torrential tropical downpour. The schooner heeled until I thought her crazy mainmast would go overboard. It whipped at the hounds and bent in an alarming fashion. Yet it survived the test and gave us more confidence in its questionable reliability.

What struck me as ominous about the vessel's behaviour in that squall was that she gathered very little extra speed, due to the enormous barnacles on her bottom. She also made a lot of leeway. Before leaving Balboa she had discharged much of her normal ballast in order to get out of a mud berth. It appeared that this ballast had never been put back, and the schooner stood high out of the water and sailed like a crab.

She was indeed a poor specimen of a Bluenose, for these Nova Scotian vessels were the smartest in American waters, and I feel sure that no British trading schooner could have come near them for speed. No seaman has ever expressed anything but admiration for these wonderful fore-and-afters from up Lunenburg way, and I had for some days been keenly anticipating my first experience of sailing in one. It was therefore something of a disappointment to find myself aboard such a slovenly and ill-kept vessel.

Sam soon tried to exert his authority over both Bully and me, in spite of the warning I had given him before we left the island. I told him again that I would have none of it and I would see to it that his life was a misery for the rest of the trip if he tried any domineering ways again. Valentine, detecting friction between us, had me down in the cabin to soothe my feelings and told me that when he was not on deck himself he would leave me in sole charge of the schooner. He also relied entirely on my navigation and, feeling unwell, retired to his bunk for days on end.

Jimmy soon established herself on board, complete with a new sand box, and under some disgrace for spending two days in the bush with a wild cat just before leaving the island. But the shame she had brought to our door was soon forgotten, and although Sam said he wanted to kill her for luck she made friends with everyone and became the old man's bedmate.

For several days after leaving the island we stood to the eastward against light headwinds and an occasional squall, so that I began to hope our passage would not be so long drawn out as I had expected. It was a dreary life, making about twenty to thirty miles a day and never a sail to shift except when we put about. She tacked poorly and to get her round we had to dowse the forestaysail and haul the mainsail out to windward with the preventer tackle.

The schooner's lack of food caused us all a good deal of anxiety, and even in the first week of the passage our diet was confined to a plate of rice in the mornings and a plate of butter beans in the afternoon. This was supplemented by so-called "Johnny cakes", which consisted of dough fried in coconut oil, somewhat heavy on the stomach and conducive to prolonged constipation, but nevertheless they were eaten with relish.

I ventured to suggest to Valentine that the crew be put on a water ration of three cupsful a day with only one meal, all the rice having been eaten in the first few days. This he agreed to, and our real trials began. We kept out of the sun as much as possible, and frequently drenched ourselves with buckets of sea water to ward off the bugbear of thirst. Braun, who did most of the cooking, started on our last bag of beans and found it spoiled by maggots.

Slowly the old ship edged her way nearer and nearer the coast of Costa Rica. I asked the skipper for permission to make a tack to the northward and he consented readily. Braun and Sam were for ever asking me how far we were from land. Each day, to encourage them, I had to say that we were a little nearer, even though we had often drifted back in the prolonged calms. But of course this could not go on for ever, and I prayed for wind so as to raise the land and convince these two. disconsolate souls that we were at last getting somewhere.

Some days out from Cocos, Bully set about the engine, and three days of very hard work were crowned with success. Every part of it he had dismantled. Covered with oil and grease, he swung the handle at the end of his work and was rewarded with a heartening roar and a rattle of ancient machinery. At last we felt that we had the means of getting into port.

The skipper, enormously cheered, asked Sam how much petrol we had.

"About forty gallons, sir."

"That'll take us forty miles," said the skipper, "so if we can make Cape Mala we'll use it to punch the current up to Taboga island or thereabouts."

We all felt much encouraged, and the excitement on board was intense when at dusk that night, our fourteenth day at sea, we sighted the light of Jicarita. This Jicarita is a small island off the southern shore of the larger island of Quibo or Coiba (the Isle of Snakes).

Into Damas Bay at Quibo there runs a fresh-water stream and I suggested to the captain that we anchor there and replenish the tanks before going any further. He considered this for a time but decided, now that we had the engine to fall back on, to carry on for Cape Mala. He therefore ordered the schooner to be put about and with a gentle breeze we bore away to the south-east.

The skipper began to spend more time on deck, and the more I saw of him the more I liked him. In his quiet moments he revealed himself as a man of sensitive nature and generous disposition. The sympathy he expressed with Bully and me over the loss of our vessel came, I felt certain, from genuine feeling. He said that he was very glad of our help in getting the vessel back to Panama and only wished that we had been able to join him running the trades down to Nuka Hiva. He seemed anxious to help us when we reached port and talked over many schemes he had conjured up from time to time. One was that I should skipper the schooner, with Bully as mate-engineer, and take her out on charter while he and his father went back to the States. Another idea was that we should sign on as crew for a voyage up through the Indies or perhaps down the west coast of South America, after the vessel had been overhauled. But nothing was definite.

I felt sorry for Valentine, for he was obviously suffering from some nervous disorder which at times made him unbearably irritable. The stump of his leg was also giving him trouble and it was essential that he should get to a hospital as quickly as possible. It was therefore even more harrowing for him than for the rest of us to be so long delayed by calms and a sluggish ship.

On the morning after sighting Jicarita light there was no sign of land. Braun and Sam were rather disheartened by this, for they had hoped to cheer their drooping spirits by a view of the coast at dawn. The breeze hauled to the east and soon we could not make a better course than south. However, the skipper thought it best to stand on thus and trust to rain for the replenishment of our now almost empty water tanks.

Three days after sighting the light, three days of calms and light headwinds, Braun announced that we had but four gallons of water left. And this, from the bottom of the main tank, was brackish and dirty. Sam was ordered to go round every tank and keg on board and sound for the slightest drain of fresh water, but his report was only what we expected.

"Every God-damned thing dry, Captain."

So now it was only one cupful a day, and we continually poured sea water over our heads and bodies when working on deck in the burning sun. The skipper and I calculated that if we used three pints a day between the six of us, and one quart a day for cooking the beans, we could last out another seven days.

Soon the dirty water and lack of fresh food began to make itself evident. Sam's black skin became speckled with white spots such as I had never seen before; and the skipper looked dreadfully ill. Braun and Bully were the healthiest looking, for I had broken out with sores and signs of scurvy. I felt like a leper.

We adopted a system whereby each man could take his water ration whenever he liked under the skipper's supervision, and most of us felt that the easiest way was to drink half a cup in the forenoon and another half cup at night.

Old Man Valentine bore up like a hero, and although he became even thinner and more haggard-looking he never voiced a word of complaint. Braun, too, kept cheerful under the strain and even rose to cracking a few of his Chicago quips to keep the party in the best of spirits. Bully, as might be expected, took the whole business as a matter of course and went about his duties as though he were in a well-found and well-victualled vessel.

One morning the skipper called me to the side of his bunk when all the others were out of hearing and told me to go and inspect all the water containers myself without letting anyone know what I was about. This rather mystified me, for I felt sure that Sam would not have overlooked the slightest drop. So I waited until my night watch and went round with a ruler and thrust it into all the tanks we had brought from the beach. Every one was bone dry. Then I went on to the foredeck. Here were two fifteen gallon kegs made fast in chocks and presumed to have been emptied long ago. The starboard one was empty, but to my delight the port one contained at least two gallons of water.

I woke the skipper and told him of my discovery.

"Put it in the big tank," he said, and grinned as though his suspicions had been justified.

We caught sharks and a lot of dolphin. The dolphin were particularly good eating and we either fried them in coconut oil, of which we had very little left, or we steamed portions over a pot of boiling sea-water. Although the dolphin flesh was a welcome addition to our diet of beans, we soon found that it made us more thirsty. We, therefore, ate only small pieces, and only Jimmy had her fill. Jimmy often meowed pitifully for water, and would sit for hours in front of the tap, so that Bully and I were constrained to give her a saucerful out of our own ration. In addition the skipper, who could not bear to see an animal suffer, allowed her a few drops as a ration each day.

On April 13th my sights showed us to be forty-five miles from Jicarita and seventy miles from David Bay, the only other place where we could hope to get water and provisions. The skipper and I therefore came to the conclusion that we should put the schooner on the starboard tack and try to make the land again. There was a faint hope that we would fetch up to somewhere near Cape Mala, and then .we thought we could use the engine to push round in to the Gulf of Panama. So each day I had to assure Sam and Braun that we would soon see land again.

For a time we seemed pinned south by the current to six degrees fifty minutes or thereabouts, and after two days on the starboard tack we had only made one mile to the north. And because the vessel made leeway like a crab our longitude failed to improve, so that soon I began to doubt our ability to make Jicarita again without a fair wind.

As I was at the wheel one morning a great whale broke surface a few yards from our stern, far too close for my peace of mind. He blew and dived and came up again just ahead of us. So near was he that I began to wonder if there was any danger of him coming up underneath us and giving our unstable planking a lash with his tail. I called the skipper and as soon as he saw how close the whale was he shouted for Braun to bring his rifle.

Each time a bullet hit the whale he dived, but he seemed loath to leave us; so Valentine waited for a chance to see his head. As soon as the snout showed above water the skipper fired — and the next time we saw the whale he was some two miles off.

Not long after the whale had gone the southern horizon became clouded with a squall. There was rain in it, and every chance of its striking the schooner. Bully and Sam hurried out on deck and rigged a large awning over the cabin top.

The squall was ours all right, and the rain came down in torrents. While I steered the others worked frantically, draining off the water into biscuit tins, tanks, barrels, saucepans and anything they could find. It was all over in a few minutes, but we counted up forty gallons of water after the sky had cleared.

Each man was given a full half-pint of water to celebrate and that evening we had a comparatively luxurious meal of beans, dolphin and Johnny cake. With the extra water, and the prospect of seeing land again the next day, we were like a lot of schoolboys.

No excitement in the social life of modern civilisation can compare with that which prevails in a waterless ship on the coming of rain. One experiences a feeling of wanting to shake hands with everyone and slap the backs of those around one — to let out whoops of joy and shin up the mast for sheer delight.

We all felt the same in the *Franklin Barnett*. There was no more grumbling, no more quarrelling. Everyone was a fine fellow.

That night Sam raised the cry of "Land ho!"

The light was not good enough to identify the coast, so, the winds being very light, interspersed with long periods of calm, we stood on towards the land until dawn the next day. As the sun rose we could see the desolate little island of Montusoa right ahead and away to starboard were the islets of Jicarita and Jicaron, with Quibo in the background.

A Friend in Need

The skipper announced his intention of going into Damas Bay, Quibo Island, to get water and perhaps a few provisions from the penal settlement there. This settlement belongs to the Panamanians and it was agreed that Sam, being the only one of us to speak Spanish, should go ashore with a letter and negotiate with the Governor or warders for the purchase of food. But all these arrangements proved to be in vain.

All about us were rainless squalls. Suddenly one of these struck us from offshore so that we had to head eastwards. As we sailed along the coast we could see the palm trees and jungle ashore and the surf breaking high over the rocky headlands. Hardly had that squall passed than another came from the same direction, and we began to fear that we would not be able to make enough windward progress to reach Damas Bay. Between squalls it was dead calm, and towards evening a turtle came lazily under our bow. Sam, an expert with a harpoon, soon had it dead on the foredeck. We got twenty-five pounds of meat off that turtle, and cursed our luck that we had not the water to make turtle soup.

Three more whales came round us, but soon sheered off; and all night we lay becalmed with the light on Jicarita taunting us between its flashes. With sunrise a hard north-easterly breeze came off the land so that we could not lay anywhere near our course for Quibo on either tack. This was no squall, but a steady wind, and finding ourselves being blown away from the islands we made the best of it and headed eastwards for Mariato, a lofty point on the Panamanian mainland. With the enormous leeway the schooner made we soon lost sight of the islands in the haze and prayed that we might soon see the land again, if only for the sake of moral encouragement. We were near the shipping lane and several times saw steamers in the distance. In view of this we became a little rash with the drinking water, having as much as six cups a day each. With the extra food we were able to cook in the form of turtle steak and our old friend the dolphin we felt much livelier and the general working of the ship was carried out in a smarter fashion.

I was taking an afternoon snooze when Sam shook me and asked me to come on deck quickly. I scrambled out and found that the foremast had gone at the hounds. Although not entirely broken off, it lay over to leeward at a crazy angle. We dropped the foresail and the forestaysail and set about hauling the masthead straight again. Sam went aloft while I spliced some new hemp for him to take over the truck and round outside the crosstrees. This jury rigging was then made fast to the lower part of the mast, for the skipper feared that it would be too rigid if brought right down to the deck. This arrangement stood the test of a squall and we felt that at least it would save the mast for the time being.

No sooner had we done this than we found that a large hole had appeared in the fore side of the mainmast. This hole was big enough to get a hand in, and I drew out a fistful of dust where there should have been solid wood.

On our twenty-seventh day at sea we came off Mariato Point and could see the great mountain reaching up into the clouds. Steamers came quite close, and with a light but steady breeze over the quarter we felt that our tribulations were at last coming to an end. But we were soon to pay for our rashness with the rain-water, for as we approached Cape Mala Braun reported only

six gallons left. This came as something of a shock, for we
thought we had plenty and to spare.

Rations again—two cupsful and a searing thirst in the heat of
the day. The only consolation was that a westerly breeze gave us
a run of forty miles from noon to noon, so that we passed Morro
Puercos and were soon abeam of the cape, heading across the
mouth of the gulf to get out of the contrary current.

Once more fortune scowled on us; no sooner did I report to
the skipper that our longitude was improving than the wind fell
away and left us in a flat calm. The current set us back and
before long we were again off Morro Puercos.

For two days there was not a breath of wind. We tried to get
inshore to pick up the night breeze without success, and at last
resigned ourselves to waiting and hoping. Our monotony was
broken by a thrilling hour one afternoon when the primus stove
blew up, for having no kerosene we had been using petrol.

I was talking to the old man in the fore cabin when I heard a
shriek from Sam, and Jimmy came tearing by with her ears laid
back. I hurred aft and found the saloon enveloped in smoke. The
galley bench was blazing furiously and Sam leapt up the
companion way with his clothes on fire. Bully was after him in a
second and threw a bucket of sea water over him as he reached
the deck. He then tore the charred rags off the screaming man
and returned to the cabin to help fight the conflagration.

The smoke was so thick that we could not find the fire
extinguishers. Braun, losing his head, threw the last of the flour
on to the fire, and it was not until the skipper laid hands on an
extinguisher that the spreading of the flames was checked.

By this time Sam's bunk was alight and the flames were
licking up through the skylight and threatened at any moment to
reach the mainsail. We formed a chain to the deck and threw
buckets of water into the cabin while the skipper lay on the floor
pumping the extinguisher. The fumes from the liquid of the
extinguisher set up a choking gas which forced Valentine to get
lower and lower until he was lying on his belly, coughing and
suffocating in great distress. I called to him to get on deck before
he was gassed, but he refused to leave his post.

For a time we just managed to hold our own with the fire, and
Bully had the presence of mind to go on deck and square off the
main boom so that the sail did not come anywhere near the

skylight. As we worked we had constantly to get out on deck for air, and I feared that the skipper would not survive if he stayed below any longer. Presently I saw him cease pumping and, gripping Braun by the shoulder, point to the companion way. He could not speak.

Refusing help, he hauled himself out into the open air and, having recovered his breath a little, called to everyone to get on deck. He saw that the flames were subdued, and with a couple more buckets of water there was nothing left but smouldering wood.

I could not but admire the fearlessness of the skipper and the coolness with which he brought the flames under control. He knew that if he for a moment forsook his post with the extinguisher the ship would have been burnt to the waterline.

We now commenced to reconstruct the galley and clear up the unholy mess in the saloon. The skipper gave Sam a lecture on the care of the primus and Braun came in for a severe cursing for throwing away the last of our flour. Poor Braun was always getting cursed for something, and under the skipper's rasping tongue and the dominance of Sam his life was sheer misery. Bully and I felt sorry for him, but even I was guilty of railing at him sometimes for the silly things he did. No amount of explanation would convince him that when doing his trick at the wheel he must watch the compass and keep a careful eye on the wind. He was supposed to wake me if the wind changed, but time after time Bully, who always had to relieve him, would come on deck to find everything aback and the schooner points off her course.

The extra food we had been having, combined with the excitement of the fire, seemed to bolster up the skipper's health, and he took the graveyard watch to allow Sam to recover from his burns. These we treated with ship's vaseline, which is usually used for greasing the masts.

One morning, when the water was nearly all gone, a small schooner came down on us from the eastward. She headed our way and Bully and I soon recognised her as the *Pasajero*, which had been berthmate with us as the *Thelma* lay off Cristobal. We sent off Sam and Braun in a dinghy to intercept her and ask for food and water.

The *Pasajero*, under her auxiliary motor, rounded-to close by and the skipper, who was a white man, asked us what was the matter. Our skipper replied that we had no water, hardly any food, scurvy in the crew and had just survived a fire. The master of the *Pasajero* scratched his head and said that we must have had a nice trip. He sent over two ten-gallon casks of water, a bag of rice and a branch of bananas. Not much between six of us, but he explained that he was only on a short voyage and had very little stores or water. And such water as he had had been obtained in Gatun Lake and bore a distinct flavour of sewage. But it was drinkable and we did not complain.

The *Pasajero*'s skipper refused to take any money for the stores and advised us that the current was running strongly from Cape Mala to the westward; also that it was dead calm in the Gulf of Panama.

After the *Pasajero* had gone on her way we decided that our only way of rounding Cape Mala was to start the engine. Sam was instructed to find out how much petrol we had left, for we had been using it extensively for burning in the primus stoves. To our horror he announced that there were only six gallons. His previous estimate of forty gallons must have been pretty wide of the mark.

Six miles progress would not have been worth the loss of the fuel, so we once more resigned ourselves to the wiles of the wind.

Day after day was the same. We would creep up to a position off Cape Mala, only to be becalmed and set back to Morro Puercos. One night we even drifted back as far as Mariato, and it was not until after two days' tacking that we were able to get up to our old bearings of what Bully renamed Moral Perverto.

The coast hereabouts was mountainous and steep and there was not the slightest hope of getting any petrol, even had we been able to effect a landing through the surf. For the country was nothing but bush-clad mountains, and a few natives were the only inhabitants.

Every day the stump of the skipper's leg was getting worse, and the exasperating calms kept gnawing at his jangled nerves. His father, on the other hand, surrendered himself to the conditions and spent most of his time in his bunk. He, too, was something of a spiritualist and would scribble incessantly on sheets of paper, telling us that his hand was guided by the spirits and that pictures would appear and disappear amid the maze of pencil marks. And since he himself was no artist he contended that the said pictures were the work of the spirits of the Great Beyond. He also showed us how spirit writing was done, but we were not very successful in obtaining messages except when we cheated.

Meanwhile the skipper continued his seances alone, and often we would see him draw a curtain across his bunk and we would hear him talking within. Sometimes, in the evening, he would even come out and sit on the rail to converse with his spirit friends in a low voice, to the awe of Sam, who thought his captain something more than an ordinary mortal.

As for the rest of us, knowing nothing of the ways of spirit mediums, we kept away from the skipper and left him strictly alone when he was in communion with the other world. He told us frankly to take no notice of him and that it was no cleverness on his part to be able to talk to the deceased, just a natural gift.

On our thirty-third day at sea a steamer came within a few miles of us to the southward and we resolved to try to get into touch with her. Dropping all but the mainsail to attract her attention Sam and I stood on the foredeck and waved semaphore flags until she came off her course and headed towards us. Valentine was now determined to get to Balboa by any means, and casting aside all thought of expense wrote out a message which he asked the steamer to send to Balboa by wireless.

The ship proved to be the *Cornwall* of London. After exchanging semaphore messages with her we heard the cadets being piped to boat stations. And very smartly they set about it, too, for in a few minutes a surf boat was lowered and came over to us, pulled by a crew of hefty lads in charge of the third officer, Mr Brown. He gave Valentine the compliments of the master, Captain Reilly, and asked if there was anything he could do for us.

In a few moments he had the whole story from us, and the boat returned to the steamer with all our empty kegs. A hose pipe was lowered over the steamer's side and the kegs were refilled in a few minutes, while sacks of provisions were slung into the boat. Back they came—eggs, bacon, salt beef, tea, sugar,

oranges, such a feast as we had not set eyes on since leaving
Balboa three months before.

The cadet crew crowded our deck demanding souvenirs, and
as delighted as we were that they were able to assist us. We
gladly gave them such things as we had saved; a turtle's claw,
shark's teeth, fish tails and the like. For Bully and me it was
charming to listen to English voices again and to be able to
converse with our own countrymen. We had not spoken to an
Englishman, apart from Graggs at Colon and Cooknell on Cocos,
since we had sailed from Trinidad the previous November. All
the news and gossip of London was extracted from them. Arsenal
had won the first division, Woodfull was to captain the
Australian Test team; Jack Doyle had faded out of boxing;
Ramsay MacDonald was still Prime Minister. It was strange to
hear talk of all these things. It seemed too much like a dream. At
last the officer called the boat away and assured Valentine that
the message to Balboa had already been sent.

As the steamer got under way again the Red Ensign was
dipped to us and we replied by lowering the Stars and Stripes.
The cadets gave us a cheer — and once more we were left alone.

There being no wind, our first thoughts were for food. Like
schoolboys at a dormitory beano we sat around drinking tea,
slicing new bread and butter and eating bacon and eggs. Sam,
knowing nothing of this grand old English dish, was hustled out
of the galley while we cooked them our own way. And so much
was he disgruntled that he refused to eat any, and kept his share
of the eggs to be boiled and spiced in native fashion.

Now all seemed to be well, for although there was not a
breath of wind the tug would not take long to come from Balboa.
We were somewhat surprised, therefore, to see in the evening a
big steamer coming towards us from the west. It was the
Cornwall again.

She hove-to and the boat was lowered—with a different crew
this time, for the others wanted their share in the fun. Mr Brown
brought two messages for us. There was no tug available at
Balboa but the S.S. *Chiriqui*, eastward bound, was standing by a
few miles to the south and would tow us to port. The skipper was
doubtful about accepting the *Chiriqui*'s offer, for while he had
reason to believe that he would get moderate terms from the
Balboa tug he could not be at all sure what he was letting himself

in for with the *Chiriqui*. The laws of salvage are very rigid.

Captain Reilly had ordered the boat to carry more stores for us because he felt that we had not been given enough before. In fact I understood that he had railed at the steward for stinginess, though we thought he had already been over-generous.

So there were more loaves and biscuits and we felt like lords as we surveyed the piles of boxes on the deck. The captain's kindness was almost embarrassing, especially considering that he had retraced his course in order to give us a reply to our message.

With the ship thus re-victualled Valentine decided that we could afford to reject the *Chiriqui*'s offer and make our own way up the Gulf, even if we took another month to do it. The season of westerly winds was approaching and we would be bound to get a favourable slant sooner or later.

So again we bid goodbye to the *Cornwall*, which was bound for New Zealand, and bent our backs to sheets and halliards as the breeze came after dark. We worked cheerfully now, and only Sam was dispirited. He had thought that in wirelessing for a tug all our trials would be over and that we should be in port in forty-eight hours. Now to find that we had a few more weeks of sailoring before us was too much for him to bear. He spoke not a word to anyone and wore a face so mournful that I was tempted to give him a good shake to wake him into activity.

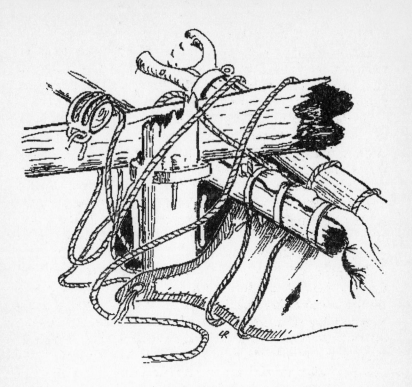

Dismasted

The day after the *Cornwall* left us we picked up a smart north-easterly breeze which, although forcing us away from the land, gave us sufficient mileage to get abeam of Cape Mala once more. At night we could see the glimmer of the light and all hands, even the disgruntled Sam, were saying that our bad luck was done with at last.

A hundred miles up the Gulf and we should be in port. Even if the wind headed us from the north and compelled us to go out round the Pearl Islands, we did not anticipate being at sea for more than another week. And there were stores and water enough for a month.

It was, therefore, a great disappointment to find ourselves becalmed again. Sam said a breeze was sure to come because he had killed another shark and its tail decorated the end of the bowsprit. Braun said he "somehow kinda felt we'd be stepping out ashore soon." There was always some fascination for Bully and me to listen to his Chicago talk.

Bully was not so optimistic. He just tallied all the food and worked out how long we could last on it. The next day, being out of sight of land, I took a longitude sight in the early morning. To my dismay it worked out to the longitude of Morro Puercos. We had already lost what little we had gained the day before. I reported to the skipper and he told me to take another sun sight in the afternoon. This caused my heart to sink even further, for we were even more to the westward than in the morning, going astern at the rate of about eight miles in six hours.

At evening a gentle breeze from off the land pushed us a little further out to sea and then left us becalmed again.

The skipper raved and swore and cursed every man jack of us in proper bucko style, and soon we were a shipful of discontents once more, quarrelling and all but fighting every hour of the day. I believe an honest up-and-a-downer would have cleared the air and left us a more peaceful crew, but this point was not quite reached.

On the morning of the thirty-seventh day, by which time I calculated we had made only 250 miles from Cocos, we found ourselves almost back as far as Mariato again and we were losing latitude every hour by a slight southing in the set of the current. There was no land in sight, not even the great peak of Mariato. So far had we drifted that we were out of the steamer lane once more and only occasionally could smoke be seen on the northern horizon.

Our hopes were raised by signs of squalls to the southward, and by midday the sky was clouded all about us. I had just come off watch when the first squall struck us. Braun took over the wheel and barely had I descended the companion way than there was a crash followed by a cracking and splintering of wood. We were all on deck in a moment.

The schooner was dismasted. The foremast had broken off at deck level and was swinging wildly backwards and forwards amongst the rigging, suspended by the jump stay to the mainmast. And in concert with this crazy swaying the mainmast rocked and cracked, threatening every moment to be torn from its already precarious stance. A tangle of spars and canvas, with the forestaysail mixed up in it as well, crashed back and forth with the broken mast.

Before the skipper could get out on deck, he not having shipped his wooden leg, we had, at no small peril, got the foresail and forestaysail on deck and out of danger of being torn to pieces. Valentine then took charge and summed up the disaster with a fine coolness and decisive manner.

"Get a line on the masthead and steady it," he shouted.

This was no easy task with the mast threatening to break our heads every time we went near it, but at last we got a strong line round it and hove the foremast against the mainmast to hold it steady. Our work was safer now, and every man was given a job in stripping the foremast of all its rigging, cranses and masthoops, while Valentine and I set about splicing and seizing new stays to save the mainmast.

At considerable danger to himself, for the rotten mainmast was likely to come down any moment, Sam was hauled aloft in the bosun's chair to get a strong warp round the mainmast hounds. This led to the bitts and we hauled it taut by the anchor capstan.

For a time, then, the mainmast was safe and we were just about to send the new rigging up to Sam when he said he felt sick. If we did not lower the bosun's chair in which he sat, he said, he would climb out and come down the shrouds. So we got him down and Valentine ordered me to the masthead to hook on new blocks, reeve new halliards and fix a new wire stay to lead to the bowsprit end.

It was desperate work, clinging on with one hand, holding rope in my teeth and working as best I could as the schooner rolled to the swell. One moment I had nothing but sea under me, then the vessel would appear to pass beneath and I would be over the sea on the other side. I could see the sharks and dolphin deep down in the water and wondered which would be the best place to land if I fell — on the hard deck or in the ditch with the sharks. But I had spent many a day in a schooner's cross-trees in years gone by and I knew the old motto "one hand for the ship and one for yourself". And experience had taught me that the "one for yourself" was most important.

In less than an hour all the masthead gear was shipshape and
Bristol fashion, and I came down on deck to find that the others
had cleared the wreckage and were about to dump the foremast
over the side. It was almost hollow with dry rot, and the skipper
rightly decided that it could not possibly be of further use.

Sam being a fair seaman on deck, and Bully keeping a level
head all the time, the work of getting the vessel under jury rig
proceeded as smartly as any skipper would wish. Valentine
hopped about on deck on his one leg, working with us, pausing
only to hurl streams of abuse at the bewildered Braun.

O.M.V. came on deck to offer his assistance but he was never
a seaman, and was too old to be anything but a hindrance. After
he had nearly been crowned by the mast his son curtly ordered
him to "go below and stay below." The old man was sensible
enough to comply with this unmistakable hint.

Five hours after the loss of the foremast, we set up jury
headsails and the work was finished. Even the skipper admitted
that to get the vessel under way with jury rig in such a short time
was a piece of seamanship to be proud of. As a reward a bottle of
brandy, which had been sent by Captain Reilly, was broken out
and all hands took so long a swig at it that there was not much
left by the time the skipper locked it up again.

A breeze came from the north-east and the watches were
reset. It was no use trying to point the vessel to windward, so all
we could do was to take the breeze abeam and head south-east.
She would have sailed reasonably well had she been properly
ballasted and clean bottomed, but as it was we made even slower
progress than before. The jib was set at so sharp an angle that it
had to be sheeted down to the stemhead. One of *Thelma*'s jibs
was set on its own luff to the bitts, and the forestaysail was
hoisted just forward of the mainmast.

That night we were becalmed again in a swell that slatted our
mainsail until we had to stow it for fear of losing the remaining
mast. With all the weight of canvas now on one shaky mast we
dare not carry a stitch of sail in a squall, and the slatting of the
calms also forced us to bring the sails on deck. And as our only
hope of wind came from the squalls we were likely to remain
where we were or to drift seawards indefinitely.

The skipper and I had a conference below.

"How long did you reckon the food would last?" we asked Bully.

"Five weeks, perhaps six at a pinch."

"And how far are we from the steamer lanes?" Valentine asked me.

"Fifteen miles."

The skipper thought for a moment and then called all hands on deck.

"Listen, all of you. We have got to get back into the steamer lanes. Every puff of wind must be used to work to the northward, even if it shoves her head to the north-west. Under this rig with nothing but squalls to rely on we cannot possibly make our way up the Gulf of Panama. We might drift around towards the south-west until we are out of food and water again. If any man sees a ship he is to call me immediately. Understood?"

This last instruction he put to us with fierce sternness, and retired once more to his bunk.

Just before dawn Bully woke me and said there was a steamer in sight. I went on deck with him.

It was deathly calm. He had dowsed all sail and the schooner was rolling wildly in a swell which was coming up from the south. Some seven miles to the eastward were the masthead lights of a steamship. We woke the skipper and soon everyone was on deck.

"Roberts, go aloft with a distress flare."

I hung in the rigging with the spluttering flare in my hand. I watched the steamer carefully; but she showed not a sign of altering course. She seemed to be heading south-west. I lit a second flare and Sam stood in the deckhouse with yet another so that we looked like a Brock's Benefit.

Still the steamer ploughed on her way and to our dismay disappeared over the horizon. No one went back to sleep. We all sat on deck talking of our chances of seeing another steamer. As the darkness faded I went aloft again and to everyone's joy sang out: "Ship ahoy. Bearing north-east."

She was a long way off but on a course which would pass close to us. As the grey morning broke I could see her put out her lights and could discern her great black shape rolling and pitching almost straight for us.

As she came near we waved and shouted and signalled to her by semaphore from the forecastle head. For a time she took not the slightest notice. Through the binoculars I could see only one man on the bridge and not a soul on deck. From her stern floated the Canadian ensign.

The skipper cursed and called the Canadian everything that was lousy. I fetched up the pistol and handed it to him with the suggestion that he attract attention by a couple of shots.

So angry was the skipper that I feared at first he was going to fire at the ship, but luckily he restrained himself and let them off into the air. Still the steamer went rolling past us and it was not until Valentine had fired five shots that the ship swung round and bore down on us. Even so she did not reduce speed and merely circled round at about eight knots as we tried to hail.

At last the steamer's engines slowed and she came back to us. We launched the cayuca and Sam was sent over with a radio message for Balboa, stating that we were disabled and needed assistance.

A burly pyjama-clad figure appeared on the bridge.

"What do you want?"

He had evidently been awakened from his morning slumbers and did not feel at all happy about it. We saw him read Sam's message and despatch a man to the wireless shack. His temper improving, he leaned over the weather dodger and called out.

"Say, where was that vessel built?"

"Sheet Harbour."

"Ah, I thought so," he replied with a grin. "I'm from Nova Scotia myself."

His ship was the *Canadian Britisher* (Prince Rupert, B.C.). Presently he reappeared and announced that the message had been sent.

"I guess they'll be right along in a few hours," he called and rang down full ahead. As the *Canadian Britisher* sank over the horizon we fell to talking of how long it would be before we were in Balboa.

Sam said he was straight away going to buy himself a quart of rum. Braun said he was taking the next ship to the States as soon as Valentine had paid him off. The skipper promised to buy me a gallon of beer. And so we amused ourselves until some five hours later I sighted a vessel bearing down on us. We soon made her out to be a U.S. Navy submarine tender. The American Navy, on passage from California to Panama to go through the Canal, had picked up our distress call from the *Canadian Britisher* and sent off a tender, the *Ortolan*, to tow us in.

The rail was lined with white-clad sailors as she came near. It was quite a time before anyone could land a heaving line over our rail, for the deck was so crowded with men that there was scarcely room to swing an arm.

"All fast" we sang out as a great hawser was taken round the bitts.

"O.K." came the nasal reply, and off we went at eight and a half knots for Balboa.

Two days later we were thrust into the Quarantine Station and caged in like wild animals with a horde of Chinese and Japanese. Only a few moments after we arrived the signal was given for dinner. We stormed the mess-room and had cleared up two large dinners each before the others had a chance to settle in their places.

As soon as the authorities saw how much we ate they let us out and told us to go back to the schooner. Here we remained for two days, awaiting the return of the skipper. He had gone ashore as soon as the schooner was anchored, to attend to the usual formalities of a vessel coming into port. He had ordered Braun to prepare supper for him in the evening. The supper went uneaten. That night the skipper failed to put in an appearance, and the next day Braun and Sam began to show their impatience to be paid off. Sam had a wife waiting for him over in Panama City and Braun was as eager as any of us to see the last of the *Franklin Barnett.*

Old Man Valentine thought his son might be visiting friends in Cristobal, and this explanation we were forced to accept when he did not put in an appearance on the second day.

Having no pay to come, and little inclined to stay aboard the schooner, Bully and I packed up our belongings and went ashore. Of the skipper we heard no more. It was reported in Cristobal that he had left for the States. O.M.V. knew nothing of his movements and, indeed, was himself stranded without a cent to buy himself a cigarette. Sam left the ship penniless and went back to his home. Braun, I learned later, got a job in the engine room of a north-bound steamer.

Bully and I gave ourselves over to a search for a boat to carry us on our way. We spent many days on foot, tramping from Colon to Rio Grande, Fooks River, Gatun and Panama, scouring the creeks and rivers for native craft. Here and there an avaricious Panamanian would offer us a crazily built contraption for 1,200 or 1,000 dollars.

We tried to buy the wreck of a South African yawl in the French Canal in the hope that we might salve and rebuild her with our own hands. But the Frenchman who owned her would not hear of less than 800 dollars, so we told him what he could do with his worm-ridden hulk and went on our way.

To find the timber to build a new *Thelma* was our only hope. We trekked into the bush to see if it were possible to cut red mangrove from the swamps to use as frames. But the swamps being so infected with fever and the deadly snakes of those parts being so troublesome we gave the project up as humanly impossible. There was nothing left but to get a job, for our few dollars had almost dwindled away.

We had made many friends in Balboa and Cristobal during our outward passage who now helped us to find our feet, and Jimmy found herself a home with one of these. Eventually the British Consul suggested that if we would care to escort home a poor unfortunate who had gone off his head in the stokehold of a ship, our passage to Liverpool would be free of charge. After a lot of thought we decided that this would be best, and so it was that early in May we embarked aboard the S.S. *Orbita* homeward bound. Our charge caused us only a little trouble once or twice, and although the ship called at Kingston (Jamaica), Havana, Nassau, Bermuda, Vigo, Corunna, Gijon, Santander, La Pallice, and Plymouth it was not until her final port of Liverpool that Bully and I disembarked with our large dunnage bags and such sails as we had saved from the lovely *Thelma*.

So we found ourselves in England again. Bully settled once more to normal life. For him the "great adventure" was at an end.

But for myself, my thoughts would linger forever on those trade wind days in the Atlantic; on the morning we sighted the mountains of Santa Marta, and the day we caught our first shark. Life on the island and those hard weeks in the schooner seem to me to be far more attractive than a soft and monotonous existence in London.

Time will never erase the harrowing grief of the loss of my gallant little vessel, but that is my only regret.

About the Author

Bob Roberts was a seaman born – he knew and understood the sea at a very early age and enjoyed the challenge. His father played an old concertina and many of the songs Bob sang were learnt from him. He soon began to play his own melodeon or squeeze box and was in great demand in various pubs as he sailed round the coast of Britain and abroad.

When I was young and a not very well paid bank clerk, I used to wander around the City of London, hoping to find my father for a free lunch. I knew where he was by his laugh. Later I knew where to find Bob by his singing.

He did a lot of broadcasting and TV and two solo appearances at the Albert Hall where the squeeze box was well to the fore. Bob always had his squeeze box stowed in the starboard side of the barge's cabin when he had the *Cambria*.

He started in barges before World War II and had lots of adventures during that time. He was in fact the last man to trade in sail in northern Europe with cargoes from hoof and horn to flour and coal and so on.

When sail finally became impracticable in the 60s he felt he hadn't finished with the sea and bought the Dutch built *Vectis Isle* from Mark Croucher in Newport, Isle of Wight and traded this little motor ship around the UK and to European ports always with his squeeze box. There was amazing evening in a Dutch port when Bob and our friend, the late Bill Martin, and the rest of the crew went ashore, Bill playing the bagpipes!

Sheila Roberts January 2003

SEA SONGS & SHANTIES

Classic folk recordings from the 1950s, with full lyrics,
and notes by Peter Kennedy

Featuring Bob Roberts, last of the sailing barge skippers with the
Cornish fisherman's chorus, Harry Cox, Ron and Bob Copper, and
other singers and seafaring folk – 26 songs from the last days of sail:

- Rio Grande
- Smuggler's Boy
- Maggie May
- Johnny Todd
- Haul Away Joe
- Banks of Claudy
- Little Boy Billee
- High Barbaree

- Stormy Weather Boys
- The Worst Old Ship
- Yarmouth Fishermen's Song
- Can't You Dance the Polka?
- Cruising Round Yarmouth
- Bold Princess Royal
- Hanging Johnny
- Jack Tar On Shore

- Mister Stormalong
- War like Seamen
- Whisky Johnny
- The Sailor's Alphabet
- Windy Old Weather
- The Liverpool Packet
- Farewell & Adieu
- The Smacksman

- What shall we do with a drunken sailor? • Caroline and her Young Sailor Bold

*'Pretty damned terrific throughout... comprehensive notes, lyrics and
photos... confirm the excellent value of this set.'*   *Folk Roots*

'A stunning collection'   *Musical Traditions*

Saydisc CD- SDL 405 | Barcode 5 013133440525| 66 mins | £10.95

Seafarer Books

102 Redwald Road, Rendlesham, Woodbridge, Suffolk. IP12 2TE
Tel: 01394-420789 Fax: 01394-461314
Website: www.seafarerbooks.com   email: info@seafarerbooks.com